MENTORING RELATIONSHIPS

Investing in Others

DR. T.S. WISE

Mentoring Relationships: Investing in Others

Copyright © 2015 Terry S. Wise. All rights reserved. No part of this book may be reproduced, stored in a retrieval system, or transmitted in any form or by any means, electronic, mechanical, photocopying, recording, or otherwise, without the express written permission of Dr. Terry S. Wise.

Scripture quotations taken from the New American Standard Bible®,
Copyright © 1960, 1962, 1963, 1968, 1971, 1972, 1973,
1975, 1977, 1995 by The Lockman Foundation
Used by permission." (www.Lockman.org)

Revised Edition
ISBN: 978-0-9860613-2-5

Published by
Servant Communications, Inc.
Kirksville, Missouri 63501

Cover picture © Shaffandi | Dreamstime.com - Silhouette of Two Friends Sitting on Wood Bench Near Beach.
Used with permission.

Cover & Interior Design: Lissa Auciello-Brogan

Printed in the United States of America.

14 13 12 11 10 / 10 9 8 7 6 5 4 3 2 1

DEDICATION

This book is dedicated to Gordon and Rita Jensen, former missionaries to Indonesia, who returned stateside to pastor the Northgate Alliance Church in Ottumwa, Iowa, my home town. Shortly after their arrival, our family began attending the church. Though I was only in sixth grade at the time, Gordon led me to faith. I will never forget that moment and am eternally grateful for their faithful ministry while our paths crossed in God's perfect timing.

Young people are always looking for faithful role models, and Gordon modeled his faith well. I *was* watching and even today, after years of seasoned ministry and executive leadership, I know of no other person who so richly exemplifies what it means to follow the Lord. Thanks, Gordon, for investing your life in me and being such a wonderful mentor. Any impact I have been privileged to accomplish for the kingdom of God is lovingly shared with the Jensen's.

CONTENTS

1 | INTRODUCTION 1
    The Rise of Mentoring 1
    Historical Background 4
    Biblical Background 5

2 | THE IMPORTANCE OF RELATIONSHIPS 13
    Progress and Relational Transitions 13
    Relationships: A Biblical Priority 17
    Renewed Interest in Mentoring 18

3 | WHAT IS MENTORING? 23
    Mentoring Defined 23
    Mentoring vs. Discipleship 28
    Who Can Mentor? 33

4 | MENTORING IN THE BIBLE 37
    Jesus and the Disciples 37
    Moses and Joshua 47
    Elijah and Elisha 56
    Paul and Timothy 60

5 | THE ACCOUNTABILITY FACTOR 65
    Accountability and Mentoring 65
    Inspection vs. Expectation 71
    Special Note to Pastors 72

6 | INFLUENCING OTHERS 77
    Barnabas, Timothy, and Epaphraditus 77
    Characteristics of Good Mentors 82
    Characteristics of Bad Mentors 92
    Ten Commandments of Mentoring 99

Contents

7 | MENTORS AND MENTOREES 103
  Selecting a Mentor 103
  Selecting a Mentoree 110
  Three Vital Dynamics 116

8 | LEVELS OF MENTORING 121
  Intensive Level 122
  Occasional Level 135
  Passive Level 143

9 | PRACTICAL HELPS 147
  Balanced Relationships 147
  Learning From our Predecessors 151
  Everyday Arenas for Mentoring 153

10 | EXPANDING THE BLESSING 157
  Mentoring Within the Church 157
  Finishing the Race 161

Study Guide 175

Endnotes 181

Bibliography 183

PREFACE

This book is the end result of a course on mentoring I have taught for years. The consistent positive evaluations from students, I believe, is a reflection of the topic itself as they frequently remark, "This is powerful material. I could really use a mentor in my life."

There is a growing hunger and insatiable thirst for meaningful relationships in our lives. Something deep within us resonates with the concept and practice of mentoring. We yearn for it. We wish someone had invested in us, and we enjoy building into the lives of others. We long to move beyond superficial Christianity and somehow connect with one another on a deeper level. We aspire to make a significant difference for the kingdom, and mentoring is a biblical avenue for marking others in meaningful ways.

As I look back over my life's journey so far, I can identify numerous individuals who have influenced me in ways that led to personal growth and spiritual maturity. In fact, any contribution I make to the kingdom is largely the result of others' influence upon me. I am grateful to all who shared their wisdom, taught me skills, modeled behaviors and attitudes, and dedicated both time and energy to enrich my life.

Mentoring is a solid biblical concept. In the Old Testament Jethro mentors Moses, and Moses mentors Joshua. Samuel mentors Saul, and Elijah mentors Elisha. In the New Testament Barnabas mentors Paul, while Priscilla and Aquila mentor Apollos. Paul mentors Timothy, and Jesus mentors His twelve disciples. We do well to learn from those who have walked before us.

This book is about investing in the lives of others. It is about building character, knowledge, growth, maturity, and empowering others to be all they can be. Believers desperately seek to be taught, molded, and empowered to make substantial contributions to the Lord's work. This can happen when individuals begin investing in the lives of others through mentoring relationships.

Everyone can be involved in the mentoring process—even you. This book discusses the need for mentoring, the difference between mentoring and discipleship, the biblical basis for mentoring, the characteristics of good mentors, and how mentoring can be implemented in the church. I hope that, in some small way, this book will lead to your involvement in a mentoring relationship and the life of someone connected to you will be forever changed.

TSW
Kirksville, MO 2015

ACKNOWLEDGMENTS

God

I humbly recognize that any contribution to the kingdom from this work, however small, is due to Your blessing and grace. You are the Divine Mentor who conducts the orchestra of our lives.

Mentors

Grateful acknowledgment and appreciation is given to all who have invested time and energy into my own life. May God richly bless you!

Family and Friends

As always, the support and encouragement of family and friends is essential to my writing endeavors. Realizing that I am far from being a perfect mentor to each of you, I hope you are able to identify some positive ways in which I have influenced your lives.

1

INTRODUCTION

THE RISE OF MENTORING

Mentoring! This ubiquitous buzzword is finding its way into the crevices of everyday life. Business institutions employ mentoring as a means of training personnel and coaching mid-level managers toward greater responsibility. Educators not only utilize mentoring to influence classroom students, the process is extensively utilized in the preparation of new teachers through field-based student teaching. My brother, a professor of music education, designed a mentoring program for first-year music teachers.

Government agencies also make room for mentoring. The Human Resources and Administration Office of Training and Human Resource Development has created a "Mentoring Program Guide" for the Department of Energy as a way of tapping into the rich pool of government employees. The Department of Energy took its cue from several Fortune 500 companies whose formal mentoring programs helped experienced individuals share their wisdom with younger employees. The power of mentoring relationships is also appealing to the healthcare industry.

More and more books on the subject are finding their way to the presses. There is even a rising interest in the world of academia. A doctoral dissertation noted the mounting interest in mentoring by stating the following:

> Prior to the 1970's, literature on mentoring was virtually nonexistent. Between 1890 and 1980 Dissertation Abstracts International lists only four dissertations on the subject; whereas between 1980 and 1984, over 100 dissertations on mentoring are cited in the field of education alone. Gray (1986) notes that over 400 articles and research studies focused on mentoring in the years between the mid 1970's and 1986. This literature production has continued unabated. In the 4 years between 1988 and 1992, the Dissertation Abstracts computer database lists 372 dissertations that use mentor as a key word; and between January 1993 and June 1994 alone, there are an additional 153 dissertations on mentoring.[1]

Mentoring is thriving in many arenas. It is not unusual to be involved in business, healthcare, education, and government mentoring programs. While mentoring has found its way into the secular milieu, Christians are also rediscovering this exciting topic. Some falsely believe that mentoring is merely a secular concept that has been heavily "Christianized" in order to fit a religious worldview. Quite the opposite is true! The concept of mentoring is intensely biblical, arising from Scripture itself.

Christians, with their desire to please God, firmly believe that following the teaching of Scripture is a worthwhile investment of time and energy. If mentoring is a biblical concept worthy of consideration, it should be viewed as a beneficial Christian activity. Not only is this concept steadfastly grounded in the Scriptures, but it is also a highly effective practice for leaving in its wake men and women irrevocably changed. Quite simply, mentoring works!

From my perspective, time is a priceless commodity, far too valuable to be wasted on unproductive theories and methods. I don't want something that is *supposed* to work; I desire to invest my time and energy into something that *actually* works. If you are looking for growth within a highly relational setting, mentoring provides one of the finest environments I know for maximized learning. Investing in the lives of others and allowing others to invest in us reaps a harvest of spiritual benefits that simply cannot be attained in seclusion.

Along with its solid biblical foundation and its effectiveness to mark others for the kingdom, mentoring is essential in an age of staunch individualism and rugged independence. Mentoring promotes supporting each other, sharing insights and resources graciously bestowed upon us, and replacing the selfish triad of "me, myself and I" with a deep longing for relationship. Mentoring promotes *interdependence* with each other rather than *independence* from one another.

As this book shares information about mentoring, your knowledge of the subject will increase. My goal, however, is far more majestic than merely increased intellectual capacity. I hope to gently stimulate you to embrace this concept with open arms. Only then will mentoring have a chance to personally influence your life as it moves from theory to a powerful demonstration of Christ's life in you. Without personal application, new learning is merely an exercise in intellectual futility.

The apostle Peter addresses this very issue in 2 Peter 1:5–8, instructing us to add knowledge to our faith:

> Now for this very reason also, applying all diligence, in your faith supply moral excellence, and in your moral excellence, knowledge, and in your knowledge, self-control, and in your self-control, perseverance, and in your perseverance, godliness, and in your godliness, brotherly kindness, and in your brotherly kindness, love. For if these qualities are yours and are increasing, they render you neither useless nor unfruitful in the true knowledge of our Lord Jesus Christ.

New learning, in other words, is important for spiritual growth and maturity. When knowledge is added to our faith, we become fruitful in God's kingdom. It's not the mere *possession* of knowledge that makes us useful, but its *practical application*. Thus, God requires the addition of knowledge to our faith with the expectation that it make a practical difference in our lives and the lives of others.

HISTORICAL BACKGROUND

The word "mentor" finds its historical origins in ancient Greek mythology. In Homer's *Odyssey*, an insightful and learned individual named Mentor is asked by Ulysses to protect, nurture, educate, and guide his young son, Telemachus. Ulysses, a Greek warrior, is off to fight in the Trojan War and needs a trustworthy and respected individual to oversee his son's welfare.

Although Mentor is described as an old man and a shepherd of the people, Greek mythology comes to the rescue when the oversight of Telemachus becomes overwhelming. When Mentor needs help, the goddess Athena inexplicably appears in the form of Mentor himself and provides Telemachus with assistance.

The Trojan War lasts a full ten years, and it takes another ten years for Ulysses to find his way home. When Ulysses left, Telemachus was a mere boy; when he returns, Telemachus is a grown man. Mentor must have carried out his duties well, for Telemachus grows up to be a spirited young man who helps his father recover his kingdom.

Mentoring is as old as civilization itself. The values, teachings, and experiences of one generation were passed on to the next generation by way of mentoring. At one time it was the primary method of relaying knowledge and skills in almost every field. The Greek philosophers utilized mentoring extensively. To mentor students in Athens, Plato initiates The Academy, where Aristotle sits under his tutelage for twenty years. Nearly all of Plato's dialogues are exactly that—dialogues with students. The dialogical style of teaching promotes interaction among learners as a valuable method for helping students draw forth essential reasoning skills.

Sailors used mentoring to teach newcomers the art of sailing a ship. Mentoring allows craftsmen to teach young apprentices the precision necessary to become accomplished artisans. Many believe that Jesus became an able carpenter because his father mentored the trade. Mentoring was a way of life in bygone generations. It happened everywhere.

BIBLICAL BACKGROUND

Like a fine Persian rug, mentoring is intricately woven throughout the annals of Christian history. Indeed, the beloved biblical record reveals mentoring to be an integral component of human interaction.

After delivering the Hebrew community from the bonds of Egyptian slavery, God provides them with laws and statutes to govern the emerging nation. Moses, the Hebrews' reluctant leader, is the human vessel conveying God's laws. At one point, Moses realizes that he will never cross the Jordan River and conquer the Promised Land with those he has served for over forty years. Yet, prior to mission launch, he reminds the community of the ordinances given by the Lord. Going forth to possess their rich inheritance will require faith, courage, obedience, and commitment to building the nation upon the laws of God.

My son's Little League baseball experience provided me with a glimpse into the heart of Moses during this time. While certainly not on the grand scale of leading an entire nation, a heart of love and compassion for someone you care for can open the door to powerful life lessons. Prior to stepping into the batter's box, Elliott stands in the on-deck circle timing his swing to the pitcher's fastball. I am just across the fence saying, "Hey El-man, you can hit this guy. Don't go for his high fastball. All of them have been out of the strike zone. This ump is pretty liberal with the outside corner, so step up to the plate a bit more. Remember, short step, rotate the hips, extend the arms, end high. Let's do it, buddy!"

Elliott knows that I am his biggest fan, and right before the big event, I remind him of the basics. Whether it helps or not, I am unsure, but I do know that my pep talk stems from a deep love for my son. I want him to do well, be successful, and experience the thrill of hitting the "long ball" off a cocky and overconfident pitcher.

As much as the wandering Hebrews irritate him at times, Moses is their biggest fan. Unable to be in the batter's box himself, he imparts valuable words while they stand in the on-deck circle, just about to step up to the plate. Reminding them of basic information vital to the success of their Promised Land mission reveals a father's love for his children.

Moses' "on-deck" speeches are found in Deuteronomy 4:5–10 and 6:1–9:

> See, I have taught you statutes and judgments just as the Lord my God commanded me, that you should do thus in the land where you are entering to possess it. So keep and do them, for that is your wisdom and your understanding in the sight of the peoples who will hear all these statutes and say, "Surely this great nation is a wise and understanding people." For what great nation is there that has a god so near to it as is the Lord our God whenever we call on Him? Or what great nation is there that has statutes and judgments as righteous as this whole law which I am setting before you today? Only give heed to yourself and keep your soul diligently, so that you do not forget the things which your eyes have seen and they do not depart from your heart all the days of your life; but make them known to your sons and your grandsons. Remember the day you stood before the Lord your God at Horeb, when the Lord said to me, "Assemble the people to Me, that I may let them hear My words so they may learn to fear Me all the days they live on the earth, and that they may teach their children."
>
> Now this is the commandment, the statutes and the judgments which the Lord your God has commanded me to teach you, that you might do them in the land where you are going over to possess it, so that you and your son and your grandson might fear the Lord your God, to keep all His statutes and His commandments which I command you, all the days of your life, and that your days may be prolonged. O Israel, you should listen and be careful to do it, that it may be well with you and that you may multiply greatly, just as the Lord, the God of your fathers, has promised you, in a land flowing with milk and honey. Hear, O Israel! The Lord is our God, the Lord is one! You shall love the Lord your God with all your heart and with all your soul and with all your might. These words, which I am commanding you today, shall be on your heart. You shall teach them diligently to your sons and shall talk of them when you sit in your house and when you walk by the way and when you lie down and when you rise up. You shall bind them as a sign on your hand and they shall be as frontals on your forehead. You shall write them on the doorposts of your house and on your gates.

One important element in building a "God-centered, other-oriented" society involves the passing of knowledge, values, laws, and commandments from one generation to the next. This encompasses far more than the mere dissemination of facts and figures in a cold, clinical manner. A piece of chalk, an eraser, and a chalkboard is not enough. This is not to say that facts and figures are absent or irrelevant, but the transfer of knowledge and values involves much more than mere facts and figures, as seen in the relational aspects of these Deuteronomic passages. The best way to recount inspiring stories, share the witnessing of wondrous events, and teach the statutes and commandments of God is in a relational setting. If everyone taught their children and grandchildren this way, the knowledge, values, and commandments of one generation would be safeguarded in the next.

The teaching Moses has in mind involves a lifestyle and a relationship. A mindset that says, "Do as I say, not as I do" is not only hopelessly impotent, but it is also hilariously foolish. The biggest impact upon others occurs when our words match our behaviors. When our "telling" is supported by our "living," we become efficacious examples for others to observe and imitate.

Mentoring at its finest is seen in Deuteronomy 6:5–9. How will our children know if we love God with all our heart? Simply because we *say* that we do? While verbalizing our love for the Creator is important, children realize that love extends far beyond the verbiage spewing from our lips. Youth pastors will readily confirm that kids want to see a walk that matches the talk. This is not too great of an expectation, for even God desires this. Our children will know that we love the Lord when we demonstrate it, model it, and actually live it within the challenges of everyday life.

The parent-child relationship beautifully illustrates the mentorship principle. Deuteronomy 6:7 indicates that we are to teach our children "when you sit in your house and when you walk by the way and when you lie down and when you rise up." A sensible interpretation of this verse rests with the meaning of "teach." For instance, if we understand "teach" to mean verbal instruction only, then it is quite obvious that we could never stop talking—a ridiculous idea. How can we verbally instruct another when we are sleeping? If we understand "teach" to mean lifestyle instruction, then the sense of the verse becomes clear. We teach others by modeling for them a *lifestyle* that reflects a love for God, and this includes both what we say and what we do.

We often slide down the slippery slope of compartmentalization when we partition life into various religious and nonreligious cubbyholes. It is quite common, for instance, to maintain an erroneous outlook that says, "This is the compartment of what I am *supposed* to say about God to other people, and this is the compartment of what I *truly* believe about God that is never verbalized. This is the compartment of how I am supposed to act when others are watching, and this is the compartment of who I *really* am when no one is looking." This viewpoint is eternally flawed, for God is not an addition to, or a piece of, our life; He is to be our very life. In other words, there is no time when we are *not* to live a life pleasing to Him. His vibrant presence permeates every aspect of our being. It is in this manner that we are able to "teach" while sitting in our house, walking by the way, lying down, and rising up.

The biblical method of passing experience, values, skills, knowledge, and the ways of the Lord from one generation to the next is the relational process of mentoring. Examples of mentoring abound in the Bible, and a few are listed below:

Old Testament

Jethro and Moses (Ex. 18)
Moses learns to delegate from Jethro, his father-in-law.

Moses and Joshua (Ex., Num., Deut.)
Moses prepares Joshua to lead the nation of Israel in conquering the Promised Land.

Moses and Caleb (Num. 13, 14:6–9; 34:16–19; Josh. 14:6–15)
Moses grooms Caleb for duties of leadership and nourishes his faith in the Lord.

Eli and Samuel (1 Sam. 3)
Eli's own children follow a path of disobedience, so Eli helps Samuel hear the voice of God. Samuel will go on to anoint David as king.

Samuel and Saul (1 Sam. 9–15)
Samuel assists Saul in becoming king, shapes his character, and challenges him to repent of sin.

Samuel and David (1 Sam. 16; 19:18–24)
Samuel anoints David as king and offers refuge from Saul's devious attempts upon David's life.

Jonathan and David (1 Sam. 18:1–4; 19:1–7; 20:1–42)
Peer mentoring occurs as Jonathan and David provide loyalty and encouragement to one another during Saul's reign.

Elijah and Elisha (1 & 2 Kings)
Elijah recruits Elisha and tutors him in the ways of the Lord. Elisha inherits a double portion of Elijah's spirit and continues the prophetic ministry Elijah began.

Naomi and Ruth (Ruth)
Naomi contributes wisdom, encouragement, and support to Ruth and directs her to marry Boaz. Ruth becomes the mother of Obed, the father of Jesse, and the grandfather of David.

Jehoiada and Joash (2 Chron. 24:1–25)
Joash is only seven when he assumes the throne of Judah. Jehoiada, the priest, teaches him to rule according to godly principles. When Jehoiada dies, however, Joash turns away from the Lord.

New Testament

Barnabas and Paul (Acts 4:36–37; 9:26–30; 11:22–30)
Barnabas convinces the church that Paul is safe to associate with after the Damascus Road conversion.

Barnabas and John Mark (Acts 15:36–39; 2 Tim. 4:11)
Barnabas is so committed to building into the life of John Mark that he is willing to part ways with Paul. Later, Paul views John Mark as a useful coworker, and many believe he is the author of the Gospel of Mark.

Priscilla, Aquila and Apollos (Acts 18:1–3, 24–28)
Priscilla and Aquila serve as spiritual tutors to Apollos at Ephesus. Apollos becomes a powerful spokesman for the early church.

Paul and Timothy (Acts 16:1–3; Phil. 2:19–23; 1 and 2 Tim.)
Paul becomes the spiritual father of Timothy, who joins him on one of his missionary journeys. Timothy later becomes the pastor of a church in Ephesus.

Paul and Titus (2 Cor. 7:6, 13–15; 8:17; Titus)
Paul and Barnabas win Titus to the Lord and enlist him as a traveling companion. Titus becomes a pastor and, according to tradition, the first bishop of the island of Crete.

Jesus and the Disciples (Gospels)
During Jesus' three-year ministry, He builds into the lives of His disciples by teaching them, encouraging them, and modeling a spirit-filled life. This small band of men drastically change the world as Christianity grows and spreads.

Though not an exhaustive list, the roots of mentoring clearly break more than top soil in both Old and New Testaments. Mentoring was a way of life in ancient days. We also observe the mentoring process in action when considering the Heavenly Father's relationship with His own children. Just as Mentor seeks to protect, nurture, guide, and educate young Telemachus, so God plays a similar role in our lives. He protects, nurtures, guides, and educates all who come into His kingdom.

A Protecting Father

Countless examples of God protecting Israel occur in the Old Testament. He protects the Hebrews from disastrous plagues and the death of their firstborn child. The waters of the Red Sea could have easily drowned them had the hand of God not intervened during the extraordinary crossing. Divine protection saves them from their enemies while conquering the Promised Land. When Haaman seeks to destroy the Jews, God uses a woman named Esther to protect His people. The murderous envy of Saul jeopardizes David's life on several occasions, yet David lives because of the Lord's staying hand.

Divine protection is not limited to the Old Testament, for we see the same safeguarding activities in the New Testament. While Paul is being transported on the high seas, the fury of a terrible storm rips apart his ship. He survives, as does the rest of the crew. At one point in his ministry, Paul is in such danger that he is lowered in a basket over the city wall to avoid certain death. The Pharisees' venomous hatred of Jesus leads to strategizing His demise. Yet, the Father protects Him. He is not to die until the "fullness of time" arrives.

A Guiding Father

Offering guidance is one of the Father's mentoring activities. A pillar of fire by night and a pillar of cloud by day lead the Hebrews during their travel out of Egypt. I would have loved to be there! When the cloud moves, they move. Finding Rebekah, the Lord's chosen wife for Isaac, is strictly by way of divine guidance. Jonah winds up in the belly of a large fish as the Lord guides him to Nineveh. An angel guides Philip to the Ethiopian eunuch for the purpose of explaining Scripture and leading him to faith. It is the prompting of God's Spirit that guides Peter to say in Acts 5:3, "Ananias, why has Satan filled your heart to lie to the Holy Spirit and to keep back some of the price of the land?" God sends an angel to free Peter from prison in Acts 12 and guides him to the house of Mary where a vibrant prayer meeting is in progress. A loving and caring Father guides His children.

A Nurturing Father

Nurturing is another one of God's mentoring activities. As the Israelites meander through the wilderness desert, there is ample food and water. Even the sandals on their feet and the clothes on their back do not wear out. In Hagar's moment of fear and discouragement, our nurturing Lord sends an angel to comfort her with these words: "I will greatly multiply your descendants so that they will be too many to count" (Gen. 16:10). In characteristic fashion, the caring God we serve places in our path, at just the right moment, people and events to encourage us during life's journey. No doubt you have experienced this yourself on multiple occasions.

Believers in Asia Minor experience intense suffering for simply living out their faith, so the Lord inspires Peter to write an encouraging and nurturing letter concerning their divine calling, their divine inheritance, and their new status as "A CHOSEN RACE, A ROYAL PRIESTHOOD, A HOLY NATION, A PEOPLE FOR GOD'S OWN POSSESSION" (I Pt. 2:9). As if to drive the point home, Peter encourages them, in I Peter 5:7, to cast "all your anxiety on Him, because He cares for you." A loving and caring God nurtures His people.

An Educating Father

Not only does God protect, guide, and nurture His children, He educates them as well. The Old Testament Law and Prophets are given so the people of God might learn His ways. Today, we possess the Bible, a tangible collection of sixty-six books we can see and touch. It is not uncommon for believers to consult Scripture for instruction and clarity on various matters.

Although mentoring is experiencing increased awareness and support, it is really nothing new. Mentoring has been around a very long time, as seen with Mentor and Telemachus in ancient Greek Mythology. Mentoring, however, extends even farther back in time and is firmly anchored to Scripture. When considering the way God cares for His very own children, we behold His mentoring actions (protecting, guiding, nurturing, educating).

Earlier, it was mentioned that mentoring is on the rise. What is it about our culture that lends itself to mentoring? Why is there such a great need for mentoring in our age of advanced sophistication and progress? The next chapter may help to answer these questions.

2

THE IMPORTANCE OF RELATIONSHIPS

PROGRESS AND RELATIONAL TRANSITIONS

I applaud the positive aspects of progress. Forget the old kerosene lamp. Now, with just a flick of the switch, electricity flows and instant illumination occurs. My college papers were typed on an archaic electric typewriter, and correcting mistakes often became an education in itself. Today, my computer makes life on the keyboard so much more efficient. Remember the messy mimeograph machine? With copy machines and digital printers there is no more mess, no more dirty hands, and no more ugly looking church bulletins (well, we haven't progressed that far!).

If I was a young conscript without glasses in the ancient Roman army, everything would be one big blur to me. It is not unrealistic to imagine a warrior's razor sharp sword about to cut my head off without me having a clue what was coming, or what was coming off! With progress comes spectacles, and with glasses I have perfect vision. From the washing machine to the space shuttle, progress influences every sector of life.

Without a doubt, progress has made my life easier and better in more ways than I can count. There is one glaring aspect of life, however, where we have actually *regressed* instead of progressed—relationships. Unfortunately, the cost of progress may bring with it a relationally deficient culture where our society elevates money, materialism, and a "me-first mentality" that stifles the blossoming of interpersonal relationships. To the surprise of many, the notion of advancement is not always 100 percent positive. As remarkable as it sounds, there are some things about progress that may actually bring us backwards. Though we have improved in many areas, in others we may have actually regressed.

Relational Transitions

It is helpful to keep in mind the relational transitions that have occurred in America. The shift from rural farming to inner city urbanization and the exodus to suburbanization undermines the importance of relationships. America began as a rural society. Families lived and worked together as they farmed the land. Relatives often lived nearby, making for a close-knit extended family. Everything they did, they did together. This arrangement was conducive to the burgeoning of relationships. Character could be forged, obligation and duty modeled, and skills and knowledge passed on to sons and daughters. Radio, television, movie theaters, two-income families, and crisscrossing the globe for work simply did not exist to compete for one's time. Families had each other, and that was good enough for them.

The industrial revolution brought about urbanization. Families left the farm and moved to the city seeking work in the factories. Instead of being at home and farming the land, dad went off to the factory, leaving mom behind with household and childrearing duties. Families were no longer living and working together as a single unit. Relationships deteriorated as extended families moved farther and farther apart.

Things didn't get better with a move to the urban city, and another transformation was in the making—a shift from urbanization to suburbanization. A mass exodus from the concrete jungle to the lush green lawns of the suburbs was occurring. But even this move was not without consequences as the rise of two-income families increased. Although families maintained the same level of income as their predecessors, it now takes both husband and wife to accomplish this feat. There are now more women in the workforce than at any other time. Dad is no longer the only one traipsing off to work, and the children are left alone until both parents come home exhausted.

This brings up interesting questions. If mom and dad are both at work, who is watching the children? When do mom and dad find time to be together? When do parents and children find time to interact? When they are able to be together, what is the quality of that experience if both parents are exhausted from the commute, the fifty-hour work week, and the stress of making enough money to live in the plush suburbs?

The actual time families spend together is severely impaired. I have read that quality spouse-to-spouse time averages as little as four minutes a day of meaningful conversation while quality parent-to-child time fluctuates between thirty seconds and five minutes a day, depending on which research study you read. Baby-boomers, baby-busters, the X and Y generations—where will it end? Generations raised in front of television screens and a plethora of technological gadgets are constantly bombarded with multimedia images. High-definition video games may enhance eye-hand coordination, but being mesmerized by a counterfeit world does little to enhance social interaction. The onslaught of technology may link us all together, but it may not do as much for deepening interpersonal relationships.

RELATIONAL TRANSITIONS

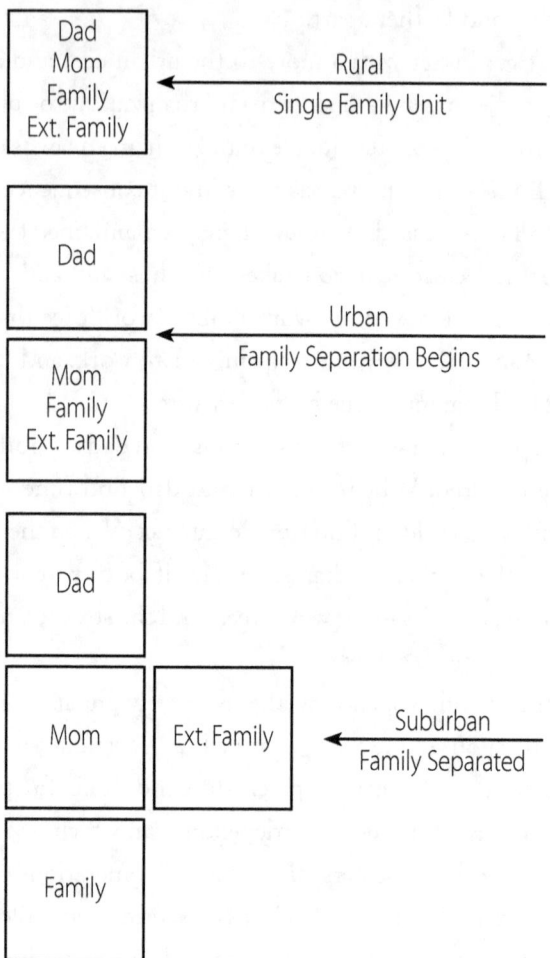

This is not a diatribe against working adults, living in the suburbs, or enjoying television and technology. My point is that the rural-urban-suburban transition negatively affects the amount of time we spend together in relationship with one another. In many ways, the mentoring philosophy is challenged because we simply do not have time for it. Progress means that other things compete for our attention, and all too often, relationships get pushed to the back burner.

In like manner, the educational milieu is in the process of slipping away from relationally based instruction. Post-secondary education in the modern age is experiencing a blitzkrieg of computers, virtual classrooms, live video streaming, and self-directed online learning, while face-to-face interaction is fighting to keep up. Some argue that relational connections between the knowledge-giver and the knowledge-receiver is weakened. I am a strong proponent of educational delivery models that promote accessibility without disconnecting students from each other and their instructor. There are ways this can successfully be accomplished, but it may not be as easy or preferred as a face-to-face encounter.

RELATIONSHIPS: A BIBLICAL PRIORITY

If relationships are low on our cultural priority list, then maybe they are not that important after all. We may be making a mountain out of a mole hill—a big deal out of something that is both irrelevant and insignificant. Why worry about the trivial?

The answer is found in Scripture. What weight does the Bible place upon relationships? Does social interaction maintain a low priority in the kingdom of God, or is it something we should wholeheartedly embrace? Matthew 22:34–40 answers that question:

> But when the Pharisees heard that Jesus had silenced the Sadducees, they gathered themselves together. One of them, a lawyer, asked Him a question, testing Him, "Teacher, which is the great commandment in the Law?" And He said to him, "'YOU SHALL LOVE THE LORD YOUR GOD WITH ALL YOUR HEART, AND WITH ALL YOUR SOUL, AND WITH ALL YOUR MIND.' This is the great and foremost commandment. The second is like it, 'YOU SHALL LOVE YOUR NEIGHBOR AS YOURSELF.' On these two commandments depend the whole Law and the Prophets."

Amazing, isn't it, that the "whole Law and the Prophets" is summed up in six verses by our relationship to God and others. If we could capture the bare essence of Scripture in a clear bottle for all to see, our gaze would intently fall upon people loving God and loving each other. It would be a spectacular sight and would speak volumes about the relational, loving God we serve.

Of premium importance is our personal relationship with God. In fact, Jesus quotes Deuteronomy 6:5 in response to the lawyer's question, "Teacher, which is the great commandment in the Law?" by expanding His answer and declaring a second great commandment. Though the questioner does not ask about a second great commandment, Jesus feels that one complements the original question so beautifully that He is compelled to share it.

Realizing the utter absurdity of loving God without loving others, Jesus quotes a portion of Leviticus 19:18: "You shall love your neighbor as yourself." Of all the commandments Jesus could have quoted, He purposely links Leviticus 19:18 with Deuteronomy 6:5, allowing us to catch the magnitude of His reply to the inquisitive lawyer.

When reading, "On these two commandments depend the whole Law and the Prophets," the basic teaching of the Bible is quite easy to grasp. It is possible to spend a lifetime studying Scripture and mine only a portion of its deep truths. Yet, Jesus has given us a summary statement on the heart of the matter. Though it is simple to grasp intellectually, it is far more difficult to practice.

What God is most concerned about is our relationship with Him and others. Many have referred to this as our vertical relationship with the Creator being lived out on the horizontal plane of relationship with others. From Matthew 22:34–40 alone, it is abundantly clear that God places extraordinary value upon the relational aspects of life. Mentoring is based on relationships, and relationships are an important trademark of Christianity. It is wholly inconceivable that one could love God without loving other people. Like Siamese twins connected at the breastbone, Jesus inseparably links the two together. Our love for God tangibly expresses itself in a love for others.

RENEWED INTEREST IN MENTORING

In light of the relational shift and cultural emphasis away from "togetherness," one might conclude that mentoring is forever lost to a selfish generation more concerned with high-tech gadgets than community obligations. Yet, mentoring is on the rise. What accounts for this curious upsurge? Why are more and more individuals seeking someone to mentor them? Why are many looking for someone in whom they can invest their knowledge? There are many reasons for this swelling excitement.

Realizing the Value of Mentoring

First, individuals are beginning to recognize the priceless impact mentoring can have upon their lives. Waking from a deceitful slumber of passivity, many are eager to enter into intentional processes of learning and maturing that require relationship with others. Yet, realizing that learning and maturing necessitates an investment of time and commitment to relationships is a new revelation to others.

Homeschooling is a prime example of expanded growth. Though largely associated with the church, a fair percentage of homeschoolers have no religious motivation for pursuing this educational avenue. One of the valuable benefits of homeschooling is the one-on-one interaction between teacher and learner. Knowledge, skills, values, and experiences are passed on in a highly relational context. This approach to learning must be working, as homeschoolers frequently surpass their traditional counterparts on standardized tests.

Unfortunately, many have never experienced positive relational environments. We may be more adept at relating to computers and machines than we are at relating to other human beings. Terms like megabytes, RAM, gigabytes, hard drive, the cloud, and windows are more familiar to us than words like friendship, relationship, sharing, caring, and relating. My point is this: if we live in a highly technical, relationally anemic society, the probability of finding healthy and positive role models may be diminished. We need relationships that extend deeper than, "Hey, how are you today?," when all along we don't really want to know. To reach our maximum potential, we need someone to look up to and someone who looks up to us.

God could have revealed Himself to humankind in any way He desired. Yet, He chose to reveal Himself in the person of Jesus, the perfect model of godliness. We get a glimpse of who God is when we examine the life that Jesus lived. As described to Philip in John 14:7–11, to see Jesus is to see the Father:

> If you had known Me, you would have known My Father also; from now on you know Him, and have seen Him." Philip said to Him, "Lord, show us the Father, and it is enough for us." Jesus said to him, "Have I been so long with you, and yet you have not come to know Me, Philip? He who has seen Me has seen the Father; how can you say, 'Show us the Father'? Do you not believe that I am in the Father, and the Father is in Me? The words that I say to you I do not speak on My own initiative, but the Father abiding in Me does His works. Believe Me that I am in the Father and the Father is in Me; otherwise believe because of the works themselves.

Peter suggests, in 1 Peter 2:21, that Jesus' own response to suffering is an example to us: "For you have been called for this purpose, since Christ also suffered for you, leaving you an example for you to follow in His steps." Paul urges the Corinthians to "be imitators of me, just as I also am of Christ" (1 Cor. 11:1). In Thessalonica, Paul and his colleagues work to provide their own living while engaged in ministry. They refuse remuneration from the Thessalonians in order to set an example as noted in 2 Thessalonians 3:7–9:

> For you yourselves know how you ought to follow our example, because we did not act in an undisciplined manner among you, nor did we eat anyone's bread without paying for it, but with labor and hardship we kept working night and day so that we would not be a burden to any of you; not because we do not have the right to this, but in order to offer ourselves as a model for you, so that you would follow our example.

Deep down inside, we long for mentors who can model what it means to be human, what it means to be Christian, and what it means to walk in righteousness. Pastors are often looked upon as models, and rightly so, but have you ever wondered who they look to as models? The casual response, "Oh, pastor is supposed to look to Jesus," is a bit naïve. Everyone, whether laity or clergy, needs someone to look up to and someone who looks up to them.

I often wonder how many bright, talented, gifted young people walk away from the church because no one took the time to build into their lives and draw out their God-given potential. Local churches are crying for wise leaders. Instead of filling leadership positions with the first person who says "yes" to the nominating committee in its frantic search for volunteers, the church could truly strengthen its foundations with mentoring programs that impact lives and guide people toward spiritual maturity. Individuals are beginning to realize the priceless value mentoring can have upon their lives.

Relational Vacuum in an Individualistic Society

A second big reason for the heightened mentoring awareness is the growing recognition that relational vacuums exists in our rugged individualistic society. Slowly, but surely, the blinders are falling off with greater numbers realizing how relationally deficient we really are.

We tenaciously cling to our personal independence. In fact, we raise our children to be self-sufficient, self-supporting, independent adults. I wonder if our quest to produce independent adults has hindered our spiritual progress. In other words, God did not create us for independence, but dependence upon Him and interdependence with each other. We are not to move through life alone with avid self-sufficiency, for this insinuates there is no need for God or others.

Wouldn't it be more profitable for all involved if we raised our children to be dependent upon God, interdependent with others, and independent of our own personal authoritative control? We arduously labor to raise independent children, but they have to learn dependence on God and interdependence with others all over again after they grow up.

A study examining over 600 leaders discovered that between three and ten significant people helped shape their lives. These individuals didn't reach prominent leadership positions by lone-rangerism and self-sufficiency; they reached the pinnacle of success because others helped them.

While a friend was driving me to the harbor in his red jeep on a sunny Seattle afternoon, the conversation turned to an accountability group he was leading. It consisted of all males who were honestly attempting to live authentically before the Lord. They agreed to share openly and honestly in order to keep one another on track. But what received verbal assent was much more difficult to practice.

One day a fellow stood up to speak, ashamed of what he was about to say, but willing to face embarrassment in order to obtain help. While sharing his struggle with sexual addition, the room fell deathly silent. The group didn't want to hear things like *that*. Struggling with the kids or experiencing stress at work was allowed, but people were not supposed to share dark matters like sexual addition. That was uncomfortable and out of bounds.

This man recognized his problem and genuinely sought support from Christian friends. He thought the accountability group was a relationally safe place to share. Instead, he was ostracized and shamed because his issues were not *acceptable* spiritual problems. This courageous man realized he needed the relational strength of others, but unfortunately, the accountability group missed a prime opportunity to assist him. Recognizing the need for meaningful relationships can be the springboard to growth, development, and spiritual maturity. Relationships become the seedlings of the mentoring process.

Mentoring is Biblical

A third reason for the upsurge in mentoring may be attributed to the discovery that virtually all training in the Bible occurred in a mentoring context. A combination of knowledge and experience in a relational environment promotes Christ-likeness. The acquisition of biblical knowledge is simply not enough to develop spiritual maturity. Knowledge must be lived out in the context of relationships that provide us with the experiences necessary for growth. Only then are we able to fully implement our learning into a mature Christian walk.

This is exactly what happens in the Bible. Jesus *teaches* the disciples and then He *walks* with the disciples. It is His method of bringing truth into the real world and making it an integral part of their lives. Far from being a new fad that quickly disappears, mentoring is a biblical method of building into the lives of others. It is a God-ordained approach to spiritual growth and maturity.

In summary, three of the many reasons why mentoring is experiencing an upsurge of interest today is because: 1) many realize the tremendous value it can have upon their lives, 2) there is an increased awareness of the relational vacuum that exists in our culture, and 3) Christians are recognizing how profoundly biblical mentoring is.

3

WHAT IS MENTORING?

MENTORING DEFINED

The American Management Association defines mentoring as:

> A developmental, caring, sharing, and helping relationship where one person invests time, know-how, and effort in enhancing another person's growth, knowledge, and skills, and responds to critical needs in the life of that person in ways that prepare the individual for greater productivity or achievement in the future. [2]

This definition grasps the effort by mentors and mentorees in moving toward greater productivity or achievement within an organization. Though it leaves God out of the picture, a wonderful definition from a secular standpoint is Webster's Encyclopedia Unabridged Dictionary that defines mentor as "a wise and trusted counselor or teacher." [3] This definition catches certain elements of mentoring, such as trust and wisdom, but lacks a broader perspective.

"Mentoring Momentum," a newsletter from the Health Care Financing Administration, defines mentoring this way: "Mentoring is the active and sincere effort designed to unleash the full potential of an individual through knowledge, skills, and organizational insights." [4] This definition, while emphasizing the unleashing of latent potential, lacks the relational aspect of mentoring. It merely states that an active and sincere effort is being attempted, which may or may not be relational in nature.

Within Christian literature, Ted Engstrom, in his book *The Fine Art of Mentoring*, states, "Mentoring is a broader term [than discipleship] describing the process of developing a man or a woman to his or her maximum potential in Jesus Christ in every vocation."[5] We now have added the phrase "in Jesus Christ," ensuring that the potential being unleashed is that which honors God.

Bob Beihl, a Christian mentoring guru, defines mentoring this way: "Mentoring is a lifelong relationship, in which a mentor helps a protégé reach her or his God-given potential."[6] Biehl emphasizes relationship, but he makes it a *lifelong* relationship. A lifetime can be a very long period of time and just the thought of such a tenure can produce discomfort. Could mentoring occur in a relationship lasting only three years? Two years? Three months?

These definitions are helpful and bring out important aspects of the mentoring process, but there is one definition that rises above the rest. In their book *Connecting*, Paul Stanley and Robert Clinton offer the finest definition I have seen: "Mentoring is a relational experience in which one person empowers another by sharing God-given resources."[7] This definition is very simple and covers the various elements of mentoring.

Relationship

Notice that mentoring involves a relational experience. If mentors are to share knowledge and experience, it is best accomplished in the context of relationship where mentors share their God-given resources with mentorees. These resources include wisdom, advice, knowledge, perspectives, principles, skills, experiences, and a host of other valuable things.

Sharing may occur over a short or long period of time, and it need not last a lifetime. It may be face-to-face or at a distance. It can be regular (weekly, bi-weekly, monthly) or irregular and occasional. Either the mentor or mentoree may initiate the relationship, but there is always one person with a need (mentoree) and one person with the God-given resources to meet that need (mentor) involved in a relationship that allows for the sharing of resources.

Empowering

Another piece of the mentoring puzzle involves empowerment. This is the driving force behind the mentoring process. Relationships become the conduit by which mentorees are empowered to move forward. With new insights, skills and knowledge, mentorees are free to become more like Jesus and expand their contribution to God's kingdom.

Mentoring relationships become fertile soil for unprecedented growth and the unleashing of untapped potential. When mentorees accept what is shared by their mentors, the power to grow is passed from mentor to mentoree. The growth I am referring to is much more than intellectual knowledge. The actual transfer of change is what mentoring is all about. If we were not looking to change something about our thoughts, behaviors, knowledge, or skills, we would not be involved in mentoring.

The term "empowerment" can be misleading if one views it as the accumulation of power. The human condition assures us that power can be improperly utilized to promote personal agendas or accumulate heavyweight influence over people and situations. This is not what is meant by "empowerment" in the mentoring context.

With mentoring, the term is used in much the same way as a computer password. The large hard drive, Internet connectivity, powerful software programs, and peripheral plug-ins are lifelessly placed on standby until the correct password is entered. The power of technology is right at our fingertips, but without the empowering password, unleashing the computer's potential is merely a dream. The key to unlocking the power of potential is empowerment.

Sharing God-Given Resources

The third essential ingredient in the mentoring recipe is the sharing of God-given resources. Some may erroneously believe the term "resources" refers to financial resources and exclaim, "So, my mentor is to share her financial wealth with me? Great! I've been looking for a way to pay off my car loan." This is warped thinking and may be more prevalent than we might imagine.

Viewing resources solely in terms of money is a serious mistake. Actually, the term is intended to be quite broad, covering a host of God-given resources. These resources may be tangible, such as showing someone how to skillfully utilize the tools of woodworking, or intangible, such as sharing insight and wisdom. Every talent we possess, every nugget of wisdom we obtain, and every skill we master is a precious gift from the Heavenly Father.

It is worth noting that the goal of empowerment *cannot* occur unless mentors share appropriate resources with mentorees. Mentoring assumes that one person possesses something of value (a God-given resource such as insights, skills, behaviors, knowledge, and so forth) that is shared with another person in need of that value. When sharing occurs in relational settings, mentorees are empowered to grow and change in ways that please the Creator.

The three core essential ingredients of mentoring involve 1) relationship, 2) empowerment, and 3) the sharing of God-given resources. This is a wonderful definition of mentoring and is precisely the type of learning environment Jesus created with his disciples.

We are learning that mentoring is God-centered and other-oriented. The other-orientation of mentoring is a powerful dynamic enabling individuals to develop their God-given potential. John C. Crosby says, "mentoring is a brain to pick, a shoulder to cry on, and a kick in the pants."[8] Mentoring emphasizes the relational aspect of learning with the goal of empowering mentorees to maximize their God-given potential.

Jesus interacts with His disciples in exactly the same way. He first establishes a relationship, then shares His God-given resources, and His disciples are empowered to develop their faith. The experience of being mentored by Jesus had such a powerful effect upon the disciples that they transform the world with their bold message. Mentoring can bring about life-changing transformation.

The disciples spend several years under the mentorship of Jesus, observing and learning how to live and serve. Their entire relationship is one of mentoring, and numerous examples can be cited in support of such activities. A bright instance of His mentoring endeavors can be seen in the washing of the disciples' feet in John 13:1–20. The disciples have yet to learn the importance of serving others. After having been with Jesus for such a long time, we wonder why the disciples fail to realize that God's kingdom is marked by service to others. Instead, they focus upon themselves.

Imagine you are outside of the room looking in through a window. You see the entire event transpire before your eyes. It is the Feast of the Passover, and Jesus will be eating His last meal with the disciples. The table is set, and all that remains is for guests to arrive.

You observe movement by the door and see that Peter is the first to arrive. As Peter surveys the room, you notice a bewildered look in his eyes as he realizes there is no lowly servant to wash his feet. Eating in a reclined position was typical Jewish practice and feet were in close proximity to others. It was not unusual and even expected that a rank and file servant would wash the feet of each guest prior to the meal. Peter was looking for the servant who would wash his feet, but no one was around. He now has a decision to make and you sense him inwardly wrestling with whether to play the servant role and wash everyone's feet as they come in or simply go and sit down. It's as if Peter realizes that a famous picture of this scene will one day be painted, and he desires a prominent seat for himself. He sizes up where he believes Jesus will sit and then carefully selects his own strategic placement. He conveniently passes over the servant role in order to obtain the best seat available.

A few moments later, another disciple arrives and goes through the same routine. There is no rank and file servant to wash his feet. Does he serve or does he sit? He notices that Peter isn't serving, so why should he? He had better secure the next best seat available before others arrive.

After everyone is seated and the Passover meal is observed, you notice Jesus rising from the table. Laying aside his garments, he grabs a towel, wraps it around his waist, and pours water into a basin. He now begins to do what none of the disciples were willing to do—wash feet. One by one, Jesus washes the disciples' feet and dries them with His towel.

The eyes of the disciples are moist as they contemplate what is happening. The guilt of self-adulation is setting in. You can almost hear Peter's thoughts,

"Why do I always think about myself first? This is a moment when I should have put into practice the teachings of my Lord, but instead I am only concerned with myself."

"What a pity," you think to yourself. "After three years of mentoring, Jesus can't get one disciple, to wash one foot, just once." These guys are slow learners. Yet, with the tenderness of a loving father, Jesus says to His disciples in John 13:12–17,

> Do you know what I have done to you? You call Me Teacher and Lord; and you are right, for *so* I am. If I then, the Lord and the Teacher, washed your feet, you also ought to wash one another's feet. For I gave you an example that you also should do as I did to you. Truly, truly, I say to you, a slave is not greater than his master, nor is one who is sent greater than the one who sent him. If you know these things, you are blessed if you do them. Do you know what I have done to you?

When given the opportunity to put servanthood into practice, the disciples fail. Rather than trade them in for another set of disciples, Jesus exhibits patience and models the expected behavior. He not only tells them, He shows them as well. What a wonderful example of Jesus' mentoring style!

Although Jesus is no longer physically in our midst, He continues mentoring believers through God's Spirit who mediates Christ's presence within us. In our journey through life, we find ourselves walking similar paths, acting and reacting like the disciples, and learning right along with them.

MENTORING VS. DISCIPLESHIP

Confusion exists regarding the difference between mentoring and discipleship. Is mentoring the same as discipleship, or is it altogether different? Does mentoring fall under the realm of discipleship, or does discipleship fall under the realm of mentoring? When teaching this subject, I often ask for a definitive response to whether discipleship and mentoring are the same. Most conclude that mentoring and discipleship are not the same, while a lesser number believe one is a subset of the other.

I view them as the same, *but* with careful explanation and clarification. I believe mentoring is really today's definition of discipleship *redefined*. We rarely use the term "disciple" today in its true biblical sense. In my mind, mentoring is the biblical expression of discipleship, and my explanation may act as a clarifying agent in distinguishing these two terms.

Though "mentor" or "mentoring" is not found in the Bible, be assured that the concept and process is clearly seen in Scripture (discussed later in the book). The word "disciple" *is* found in the Bible. An examination of this term aids in our understanding of mentoring since it contains the biblical essence of discipleship. Because discipleship is rarely used today in its biblical sense, our understanding of mentoring helps to clarify the confusion.

The Greek word for disciple is "mathetes." The verb form of this word occurs twenty-five times in the New Testament and only six times in the Gospels. The noun form, however, occurs 264 times in the New Testament, exclusively in the Gospels and Acts.

A primary hermeneutical principle of biblical interpretation is exegesis (drawing from Scripture) rather than eisegesis (reading into Scripture). In other words, it is invalid to read into or apply to the first-century text meanings from our culture and time. Correct interpretation entails discovering what the word meant at the time it was written for those to whom it was written. We must ask ourselves, what did the biblical writers have in mind when they used the term "mathetes," and what would someone who read or heard the word "mathetes" during that time period understand it to mean?

In the ancient world, "mathetes" variously designated an apprentice or one who accompanied a teacher in order to learn from him. In Classical Greek, a man was called a mathetes (disciple) when he bound himself to someone else in order to acquire his practical and theoretical knowledge. He may be an apprentice in a trade, a student of medicine, or a member of a philosophical school.

In the New Testament, discipleship is used to indicate total attachment to someone. Jesus' disciples did not assemble in formal classrooms with textbooks and final exams. They gathered in open fields and secluded places, and they learned from both the words and actions of Jesus. The circumstances surrounding those mentoring moments were as varied as the situations and locations of Jesus' ministry. The twelve disciples are learners who follow Jesus throughout his ministry with total allegiance in order to learn both theoretical and practical knowledge. By being with their Master day in and day out, they listen to His teaching, observe His life, and practice daily application of learning.

It appears that Jesus is actually mentoring the disciples. He teaches with His words, models with His actions, and empowers them for growth and development, all within a highly relational setting. The disciples seem to be more like protégés than classroom students. They are learning a way of life, not merely memorizing facts and figures. Jesus is the mentor and His twelve disciples are the mentorees, or we could say that Jesus is the discipler and the Twelve are the disciples.

Within a biblical framework, "disciple" is a close synonym for "mentor," and "discipling" is a close synonym for "mentoring." Since the word "mentor" or "mentoring" is not found in the Bible, the term "disciple," in its biblical sense, contains the concept of mentoring. If biblical discipleship is the same as mentoring, why confuse things by adding another term into the mix? Why not just stick with discipleship? Two options are available to us: 1) we are forced to re-educate people about the true biblical meaning of discipleship, or 2) we use mentoring as a means of teaching true discipleship. We eventually want people to understand the biblical concept of discipleship, but the best method of doing this may be to first help them understand mentoring, a familiar and accessible concept within contemporary society.

We utilize "mentoring" today because we rarely use the term "disciple" in its true biblical sense. Mentoring, in essence, is an attempt to get back to the *real* meaning of discipleship. If the term "mentoring" wasn't available and everyone properly understood "discipleship" to speak of one person sharing God-given resources with another so that empowerment occurs, there would be no confusion and no need for the term "mentoring." Everyone would possess the same understanding of discipleship. Unfortunately, this simply isn't the case.

In our culture, "discipleship" tends to focus on a narrow segment of spirituality. We think of discipleship as Bible study, Scripture memorization, learning seven steps to prayer, participation in a new believer's class, filling in the blanks of study guides, or attending catechism classes, just to name a few. The relational and modeling aspects that empower individuals to grow is often completely absent in this narrow approach.

When churches offer discipleship classes, what do they talk about and how do they teach? Normally, discipleship offerings occur during a Sunday School class and lasts about an hour. A teacher usually presents the knowledge to be grasped on basic topics of Christian faith. Groups may meet in homes on a week night for a more charming atmosphere, but the same methodology usually exists. Though there may be a great deal of sharing, there may also be a miniscule amount of learning. Functionally speaking, this becomes a fellowship group rather than a mentoring process. Sometimes Bible studies become nothing more than opinion-sharing events. The individual with the strongest opinion and the loudest voice usually walks away from the study thinking, "Boy, I sure set them straight," while everyone else is licking their wounds. This formal approach is what typically comes to mind when we think of discipleship.

To illustrate this point, I ask seasoned pastors to describe their discipleship or new believer's class. Predictably, they respond by describing the various topics that are taught. "Do you teach them *about* prayer?" I asked one minister. "Absolutely, we do," came his proud reply. "Do you *show* them how to pray?" I further probed. He hung his head and mumbled, "No." He got the point. Too often, discipleship is relegated to teaching in a classroom on a Sunday morning. Jesus' classroom was life itself. He not only taught His disciples *about* prayer, but He actually taught them *how to* pray. This is the vital distinction that must be made between discipleship as it is used today and its original meaning.

The problem lies not so much with the meaning of mentoring as it does with the *misuse* of discipleship. Because of this modern misuse, "mentoring" helps us clarify the true intent of discipleship. You may not buy into my position that discipleship is incorrectly used today. If so, ask several individuals within your church to list what comes to mind when they think of both terms. I have done this, and here is how it usually pans out:

Discipleship	**Mentoring**
Bible Study	Sculpting Values
Cognitive Knowledge	Modeling
Learning Spiritual Gifts	Encouragement
Study Guides	Correction
Classroom	New Perspectives
Formal	Informal
Teacher	Protégé
Student	Relationship
	Accountability

Mentoring involves much more than today's narrow definition allotted to discipleship. Mentoring allows for the development of the whole person. It involves shaping and molding people, influencing others, sculpting response patterns, attitudes, and perspectives, acquiring new habits, enlarging and expanding views of God, and increasing one's hunger to know and serve Him. It involves patient modeling while helping others grow. While verbal instruction does indeed occur, it is not to the exclusion of everything else. I look at mentoring (or the true meaning of discipleship) as a balance between instruction, modeling, and relationship.

THE MENTORING BALANCE

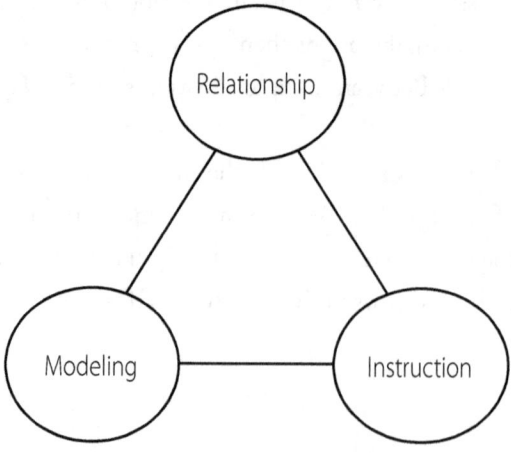

In summary, my response to the question "Is mentoring and discipleship the same?" is qualified. If "discipleship" represents the true biblical meaning of "mathetes," then my answer is, "Yes, they are the same." If "discipleship" represents the modern day, narrow, clinical version of the term and focuses on cognitive skills alone, then my answer is a resounding, "No, they are not the same."

Although this is my view of the two terms, in all practicality it matters very little whether individuals feel the terms are different, the same, or subsets of one another. I am not so concerned with what it is called; I just want us to practice it. I want us to understand that sharing God-given resources with other individuals in a relational setting empowers them toward greater kingdom impact. That's it. This is the heart of it. If you feel comfortable calling this process discipleship, fine. If you prefer calling the process mentoring, fine. Understanding the concept and putting it into practice is the heart of the matter.

WHO CAN MENTOR

Chapter 6 of Bob Biehl's book *Mentoring* is titled "Anyone Can Mentor, but Not Everyone Should." Chapter 2 of Ted Engstrom's book *The Fine Art of Mentoring* is titled "Anyone Can/Everyone Should." These two chapter titles reveal a difference of opinion regarding who is capable of fulfilling the mentoring role. Can anyone mentor, or must one possess particular qualifications? There are two schools of thought regarding this matter. One believes that distinctive qualifications are necessary, while the other believes that virtually everyone can mentor something of value.

The former views mentors as those who have achieved a superior rank in an organization, climbed the professional ladder, or have achieved some sort of notable success. Because of their hard work, knowledge, and experience, these folks are considered experts in their field. They are high-caliber individuals who shine brighter than the rest. While it would certainly be wonderful to match every mentoree with someone of this quality, it is highly unlikely for the simple reason that there are just not enough experts to go around.

The latter school of thought, however, makes more sense to me. Since there are few expert mentors who can do everything, mentoring must be brought within reach of the average person. When we say that anyone can mentor, we are not implying that anyone can mentor *everything*. It would be impossible for me to mentor someone in the area of international finance, for I have no training or experience in that realm. It would be a classic case of the blind leading the blind.

We mean to say that anyone can mentor, provided he or she has learned something from God and is willing to share with others what they have learned. This brings mentoring within the grasp of nearly everyone. The criteria are not so high that one must be an expert to mentor and it is not so low that one person mentors everything. It lies within the reasonable middle where it should be. Believers who are growing in their faith have learned *something* from God who has bestowed upon them gifts, talents, new learning, ideas, and perspectives. Mentors don't have to be experts and certainly aren't expected to swim in waters that are too deep for their abilities. They can, however, share their God-given resources with others. In this way, everyone can mentor something to someone.

Instead of one ideal individual modeling all things, it makes much more sense to have many mentors in several different areas of your life. For instance, Susan's prayer life is almost non-existent. She really doesn't know much about prayer, but she senses a need within herself to find help in this area. Whenever she thinks about prayer, Margaret always comes to mind. In Susan's eyes, there is no greater prayer warrior than Margret. Susan asks if Margaret will teach her to pray, really pray like she ought, and a mentoring relationship commences. They meet for six months on a regular basis while Margaret teaches Susan about prayer—not just the facts and figures, but actually modeling it for her, praying together with her, and sharing those moments when Susan awkwardly fumbles around for the right words to say.

Margaret may be unqualified or unable to mentor other subjects, but God has indeed taught her to pray with fervor. A relationship ensues, Margaret shares her God-given resources on prayer, Susan receives it, and new learning unleashes a whole new area of Christian life that has been neglected for years. Susan changes and becomes more Christ-like through her mentoring relationship with Margaret. She learns to pray.

Bill, on the other hand, has a serious problem with anger and impatience. He knows something has to be done about it but isn't quite sure how to approach it. Dr. Lambert, the senior pastor, would know what to do but is probably too busy, Bill thought. Then John Anthony came to mind. John is a longtime member of the board who exhibits a great amount of patience and wisdom during long and difficult meetings. When others raise their voices and jockey for position, it is John who seems to maintain control of himself and the situation. "If anyone can help my anger," Bill thought, "surely John will have some answers."

John agrees to mentor Bill in this area, and they meet together over a period of two years. Sometimes they meet regularly and other times occasionally, but a relationship is initiated. John teaches Bill the meaning of being controlled by the Spirit, gives him practical advice in certain situations, and slowly brings Bill along until he can stand on his own two feet in this area. It is a wonderful experience for both of them. Much to his surprise, a young married man named Mark approaches Bill in much the same way he had approached John years earlier. Mark is having trouble controlling his own anger and has observed Bill's transformation. Now he is looking to Bill for help. Bill establishes a mentoring relationship with Mark, and they are now working on the issue together.

You see, you do not have to be an expert. You can simply share with others those things God has taught you. Everyone can mentor something to someone. The ideal mentor who can do almost everything is few and far between and may be nonexistent. Mentoring is within reach and can be life-changing for all involved.

4

MENTORING IN THE BIBLE

JESUS AND THE DISCIPLES

This book contends, rather emphatically, that mentoring is a biblical concept, not because I say so, but because mentoring occurs in the lives of so many believers throughout the biblical text. We even see mentoring in the life of Jesus Himself. Joseph, Jesus' earthly father, is thought to have mentored the highly skilled trade of carpentry to his son. Jesus personally mentors His twelve disciples over a period of several years. They transform the world after His death and resurrection.

Upon reading the gospels, one can easily conclude that Jesus taught with His life. His mentoring of the disciples involved both instruction and example, two sides of the same coin. We never find Jesus saying, "Now class, please read Chapters 6–7 in your textbook and prepare for a fifty-minute lesson on living by faith." I am not suggesting that a fifty-minute classroom lecture on faith is without merit. As a pastor and educator, I readily support the adding of knowledge to our faith as Peter so eloquently advocates in 2 Peter 1:5–7:

> Now for this very reason also, applying all diligence, in your faith supply moral excellence, and in your moral excellence, knowledge, and in your knowledge, self-control, and in your self-control, perseverance, and in your perseverance, godliness, and in your godliness, brotherly kindness, and in your brotherly kindness, love.

It is significant, however, that Jesus' methods were much more personal than a classroom lecture. He not only verbally teaches His disciples *about* faith, He *shows* them what it means and what it looks like. For instance, He takes them in a boat to battle a storm while He sleeps. During another ferocious storm, He walks on water to demonstrate faith. The classroom for Jesus stretches beyond the traditional brick walls or online classrooms, and His view of knowledge extends far beyond cognitive understanding. Jesus desires that His disciples not only *know* His ways, but *live* according to The Way, so He gives them both *instruction* and *example*.

Teaching is one important aspect of the mentoring process, and we are not surprised to see Jesus engaging in this activity. Just as Mentor taught Telemachus, so Jesus teaches His disciples many lessons. A prime example of His instruction is found in the famous Sermon on the Mount where Matthew sets the stage for His teaching role (Mt. 5:1–2). By sitting down, Jesus assumes the official position of authority.

He initiates this powerful teaching moment in Matthew 5:3–4 with, "Blessed are the poor in spirit, for theirs is the kingdom of heaven. Blessed are those who mourn, for they shall be comforted," followed by the rest of the beatitudes. He explains the disciples' relationship to the world and to one another. In Chapter 6, He instructs them how to pray and handle anxiety. In Chapter 7, He enlightens them on judging oneself before judging others and provides examples of following the true path. He shares knowledge, principles, and wisdom with His disciples and all who come to listen. Jesus is involved in a common element of mentoring and does what mentors do; He shares knowledge, principles, and wisdom.

The warped value system of the Pharisees is exposed in Matthew 23 when Jesus says, "They say things and do not do them" (Mt. 23:3). But the kingdom value Jesus deeply believes in and teaches His disciples is that deeds and words *should* be congruous. When behavior is out of alignment with words, an incongruity exists that demeans the high kingdom values Jesus promotes. Incongruity ensnares us in the twisted value system of the Pharisees.

After revealing how the Pharisees practiced religion for the applause of men, Jesus makes an important statement regarding the value of humility in

Matthew 23:12: "Whoever exalts himself shall be humbled; and whoever humbles himself shall be exalted." Far be it from the Pharisees to humble themselves and seek humility. They practice religion for temporal human applause rather than from a heart compelled by love. They speak *about* humility but their *actions* deny any deep knowledge of the subject. Incongruities expose their true nature.

The Pharisees also exhibit a warped sense of priority. They tithe mint, dill, and cumin with exact precision but neglect the weightier provisions of the law such as justice, mercy, and faithfulness. They are all about external showmanship and lack genuine concern for their internal heart condition. God, however, is just the opposite. He is first and foremost concerned with our inward condition rather than external actions performed by means of illegitimate motivation.

In front of His disciples, Jesus tells the Pharisees in Matthew 23:25–26,

> Woe to you, scribes and Pharisees, hypocrites! For you clean the outside of the cup and of the dish, but inside they are full of robbery and self-indulgence. You blind Pharisee, first clean the inside of the cup and of the dish, so that the outside of it may become clean also.

Servanthood is another key value Jesus teaches His disciples as aptly noted in Mark 10:42–45:

> You know that those who are recognized as rulers of the Gentiles lord it over them; and their great men exercise authority over them. But it is not this way among you, but whoever wishes to become great among you shall be your servant; and whoever wishes to be first among you shall be slave of all. For even the Son of Man did not come to be served, but to serve, and to give His life a ransom for many."

In traditional Christian circles, the pinnacle of Jesus' servanthood is demonstrated upon the Cross of Calvary where He voluntarily gives His life as a ransom for many. So strong is His belief in the value of serving others that He is willing to endure a tortuous crucifixion for our benefit. The value of serving others is also detected in the impressive story of Jesus washing the disciples' feet in John 13:1–17:

> Jesus, knowing that the Father had given all things into His hands, and that He had come forth from God and was going back to God, got up from supper, and laid aside His garments; and taking a towel, He girded Himself. Then He poured water into the basin, and began to wash the disciples' feet and to wipe them with the towel with which He was girded.
>
> So when He had washed their feet, and taken His garments and reclined at the table again, He said to them, "Do you know what I have done to you? You call Me Teacher and Lord; and you are right, for so I am. If I then, the Lord and the Teacher, washed your feet, you also ought to wash one another's feet. For I gave you an example that you also should do as I did to you. Truly, truly, I say to you, a slave is not greater than his master, nor is one who is sent greater than the one who sent him. If you know these things, you are blessed if you do them."

The sculpting of values is not accomplished with words alone, but with congruity between word and deed. Jesus not only teaches the disciples *about* servanthood, but He vividly *demonstrates* it for them. He becomes a graphic, living illustration of what it means to serve others.

As a mentoring model, Jesus also encourages His disciples. Knowing that His appointment with death is imminent, our Lord encourages their sad hearts with His peace and strengthens their resolve by assuring them of the Holy Spirit's coming comfort:

> **John 14:26–27**
> But the Helper, the Holy Spirit, whom the Father will send in My name, He will teach you all things, and bring to your remembrance all that I said to you. Peace I leave with you; My peace I give to you; not as the world gives do I give to you. Do not let your heart be troubled, nor let it be fearful.
>
> **John 16:33**
> These things I have spoken to you, so that in Me you may have peace. In the world you have tribulation, but take courage; I have overcome the world."

Jesus also mentors His disciples toward deeper faith. Like stretching a rubber band, He expands the limits of their view of God. On one occasion, several disciples are with Him on the Mount of Transfiguration (Mt.17) and observe His revealed glory. This panoramic view of Christ shakes them to the core of their being.

A similar experience is seen in Luke 8:22–25:

> Now on one of those days Jesus and His disciples got into a boat, and He said to them, "Let us go over to the other side of the lake." So they launched out. But as they were sailing along He fell asleep; and a fierce gale of wind descended on the lake, and they began to be swamped and to be in danger. They came to Jesus and woke Him up, saying, "Master, Master, we are perishing!" And He got up and rebuked the wind and the surging waves, and they stopped, and it became calm. And He said to them, "Where is your faith?" They were fearful and amazed, saying to one another, "Who then is this, that He commands even the winds and the water, and they obey Him?"

Matthew 14 describes a further faith-stretching experience. In the midst of a ferocious storm, Jesus calmly walks on water while His disciples battle high waves, strong winds, and heavy rain. These events, and many other incidents, enable the disciples to expand their horizons and acquire new understandings of faith. Jesus instructs with His words and models with His behavior. His followers learn valuable insights, new knowledge, and fresh perspectives that broaden their faith and enrich their lives.

Jesus also modeled responsibility, leadership, and direction. The feeding of the 5,000 is an excellent example of leadership and responsibility working together (Jn. 6:1–14). A huge crowd follows Jesus across the Sea of Galilee to hear Him teach, and it is soon time to eat. The disciples are at a loss. How does one go about feeding such a large group without a catering service and weeks of preparation? This, of course, is a wonderful test of faith for the disciples. Will they take responsibility, display leadership skills, and step up to the plate? Seizing the mentoring moment, Jesus inquires, "Where are we to buy bread, so that these may eat?" (Jn. 6:5).

A faith opportunity arises for Philip to say, "Well, there are no restaurants out here, but these people do need to eat. I have faith that the Heavenly Father will provide a way." Unfortunately, this is not how Philip responds. Instead, he replies in John 6:7, "Two hundred denari worth of bread is not sufficient for them, for everyone to receive a little." The situation calls for responsible spiritual leadership and Philip can only think of the *impossibilities*.

Peter's brother, Andrew, pipes up, "There is a lad here who has five barley loaves and two fish, but what are these for so many people?" Right in front of Andrew is the substance of a miracle, but he cannot see it. The disciples are at a loss in what to do and how to proceed, so Jesus steps in and provides leadership and direction in a situation that demands action. He asks the multitude to sit down and instructs the disciples to distribute the loaves and fish in an orderly manner. When the multitude has had its fill, the disciples gather up the leftovers. Five barley loaves and two fish sure go a long way when faith is involved! It is a two-out, bases-loaded situation and someone needs to step up to the plate and hit a game-winning single. The situation calls for leadership and direction, and Jesus models both for His followers.

Sometimes mentors have a tendency to "play it safe" for the sake of their position. In protecting their image as the "knowledgeable one," they may lose out on valuable mentoring moments because they never place themselves in vulnerable situations. When I speak of vulnerable situations, I am not referring to compromising situations of sin. I am simply referring to a willingness to place oneself in circumstances where faith and risk can be modeled and taught.

Jesus mentors "risk taking" to His disciples. At times, He purposely places Himself in situations of risk to integrate and model kingdom values. The strength of our Lord lies in His relationship with the Father, not in the accumulation of power, the thrill of prestige, the Broadway lights of fame, or the opinion of others. His life is ruled by the Spirit of God who leads Him into vulnerable situations in order to deepen the knowledge and faith of His disciples. A scriptural example of vulnerability may help clarify this concept.

As Jesus travels from Judea to Galilee, a moment of risk arises in John 4. His journey takes Him through Samaria, an area despised by the Jews. Samaritans are a scorned people—half-breeds looked down upon by "pure" Jews. In addition to their impure ethnic identity, Samaritans are also religious nonconformists. Instead of traveling to Jerusalem for worship, they established their own worship on Mt. Gerizim. Although they believe in Moses and the Law, they disregard the prophets. This is unacceptable from a Jewish perspective.

The fact that Jesus converses with a Samaritan woman while stopping for refreshment is unheard of. Women had very little power or standing in ancient times. In fact, male Jews frequently thanked God for three things as they prayed: that they weren't born a Gentile, a woman, or a slave. Jesus intentionally places Himself in a precarious position ethnically, religiously, and culturally. Yet, He is willing to do so in order to teach His disciples an important truth. The account is told in John 4:3–42:

> He left Judea and went away again into Galilee. And He had to pass through Samaria. So He came to a city of Samaria called Sychar, near the parcel of ground that Jacob gave to his son Joseph; and Jacob's well was there. So Jesus, being wearied from His journey, was sitting thus by the well. It was about the sixth hour.
>
> There came a woman of Samaria to draw water. Jesus said to her, "Give Me a drink." For His disciples had gone away into the city to buy food. Therefore the Samaritan woman said to Him, "How is it that You, being a Jew, ask me for a drink since I am a Samaritan woman?" (For Jews have no dealings with Samaritans.) Jesus answered and said to her, "If you knew the gift of God, and who it is who says to you, 'Give Me a drink,' you would have asked Him, and He would have given you living water." She said to Him, "Sir, You have nothing to draw with and the well is deep; where then do You get that living water? You are not greater than our father Jacob, are You, who gave us the well, and drank of it himself and his sons and his cattle?" Jesus answered and said to her, "Everyone who drinks of this water will thirst again; but whoever drinks of the water that I will give him shall never thirst; but the water that I will give him will become in him a well of water springing up to eternal life."
>
> The woman said to Him, "Sir, give me this water, so I will not be thirsty nor come all the way here to draw." He said to her, "Go, call your husband and come here." The woman answered and said, "I have no husband." Jesus said to her, "You have correctly said, 'I have no husband'; for you have had

five husbands, and the one whom you now have is not your husband; this you have said truly." The woman said to Him, "Sir, I perceive that You are a prophet. Our fathers worshiped in this mountain, and you people say that in Jerusalem is the place where men ought to worship." Jesus said to her, "Woman, believe Me, an hour is coming when neither in this mountain nor in Jerusalem will you worship the Father. You worship what you do not know; we worship what we know, for salvation is from the Jews. But an hour is coming, and now is, when the true worshipers will worship the Father in spirit and truth; for such people the Father seeks to be His worshipers. God is spirit, and those who worship Him must worship in spirit and truth." The woman said to Him, "I know that Messiah is coming (He who is called Christ); when that One comes, He will declare all things to us." Jesus said to her, "I who speak to you am He."

At this point His disciples came, and they were amazed that He had been speaking with a woman, yet no one said, "What do You seek?" or, "Why do You speak with her?" So the woman left her waterpot, and went into the city and said to the men, "Come, see a man who told me all the things that I have done; this is not the Christ, is it?" They went out of the city, and were coming to Him.

Meanwhile the disciples were urging Him, saying, "Rabbi, eat." But He said to them, "I have food to eat that you do not know about." So the disciples were saying to one another, "No one brought Him anything to eat, did he?" Jesus said to them, "My food is to do the will of Him who sent Me and to accomplish His work. Do you not say, 'There are yet four months, and then comes the harvest'? Behold, I say to you, lift up your eyes and look on the fields, that they are white for harvest. Already he who reaps is receiving wages and is gathering fruit for life eternal; so that he who sows and he who reaps may rejoice together. For in this case the saying is true, 'One sows and another reaps.' I sent you to reap that for which you have not labored; others have labored and you have entered into their labor."

From that city many of the Samaritans believed in Him because of the word of the woman who testified, "He told me all the things that I have done." So when the Samaritans came to Jesus, they were asking Him to stay with them; and He stayed there two days. Many more believed because of His word; and they were saying to the woman, "It is no longer because of what you said that we believe, for we have heard for ourselves and know that this One is indeed the Savior of the world."

That Jesus would purposefully pass through Galilee to speak with a despised Samaritan woman is an astounding example of His willingness to assume risk. Others marvel at His audacity and are somewhat perplexed. In many ways, it is almost beyond comprehension. Jesus is engaging in politically incorrect behavior outside the range of acceptable Jewish norms. Though the disciples may have experienced embarrassment over the encounter, they learn a great deal about the kingdom of God, the heart of Jesus, and their own ignorant perspectives.

This despised half-breed, a woman from the wrong side of the tracks, becomes the first person to whom Jesus publicly reveals His messiahship. That alone is a sobering thought! When the woman informs the town of Sychar what she has seen and heard, Jesus seizes the opportunity. The result of His vulnerability is that an entire city believes. This is a powerful lesson for the disciples.

It should be noted that Jesus affirms both genders. Although there are no women among the Twelve, many are faithful followers, like Mary and Martha, and it is a woman who first reports His resurrection from the grave. It is the despised Samaritan woman to whom Jesus first publicly reveals His identity. Mentoring is for all persons, regardless of gender. Male or female, you can mentor and be mentored.

There are many instances where our Lord places Himself in precarious situations in order to teach His disciples, such as when He eats grain and heals a withered hand on the Sabbath (Mk. 2–3). Of course, enraged Pharisees take offense that Jesus is not obeying the law. He is "working" when He should be resting on the Sabbath. Jesus' response in this vulnerable situation is magnificent.

With regard to eating grain, Jesus states in Mark 2:27–28, "The Sabbath was made for man, and not man for the Sabbath. So the Son of Man is Lord even of the Sabbath." With regard to healing, Jesus replies to the Pharisees in

Mark 3:4, "Is it lawful to do good or to do harm on the Sabbath, to save a life or to kill?" The disciples watch and learn under the critical eye of the Pharisees.

In addition to *teaching* knowledge and values, modeling leadership, and risking vulnerability, Jesus also *trusts* His mentorees with what He has given them. He entrusts responsibilities to His disciples that require utilization of new learning. Resembling shy boys asking out their first date, the disciples often feel unprepared for the tasks awaiting them. Like baby birds, Jesus gently nudges them from the safety of their nest toward a new world of flight. It is time to implement new learning in actual real life, everyday situations.

After instructing His disciples in Matthew 10, Jesus sends them out in ministry. Later, He instructs the seventy (Lk. 10), and they go forth in pairs. Finally, in Matthew 28:18–20, He sends all of His followers out into ministry:

> And Jesus came up and spoke to them, saying, "All authority has been given to Me in heaven and on earth. Go therefore and make disciples of all the nations, baptizing them in the name of the Father and the Son and the Holy Spirit, teaching them to observe all that I commanded you; and lo, I am with you always, even to the end of the age."

Jesus is no longer sending out twelve or seventy; He is sending out every one of us as His ambassadors. He trusts you and me with His teaching in the same way He trusted the disciples in Matthew 10 and Luke 10. Though He has since bestowed the Spirit upon us, the fact remains that by sending us out He is trusting us with His teaching.

It is essential to recognize that all of Jesus' mentoring activities are carried out in a relational context. The various mentoring functions Jesus engages in involve spending time with His disciples. They are with Him on the mountain and in the valley, in the city and in the countryside, on the water and on the land, staying in a home and walking through a field of grain. They observe His life, actions, reactions, attitudes, and behaviors. They find this mentoring relationship empowering. Their faith is stretched beyond imagination, and they are encouraged. As a result of modeling a way of life for them, they turn the world upside down and Christianity spreads rapidly. Jesus certainly provides us with a grand example of mentoring.

MOSES AND JOSHUA

While we note Jesus' mentoring activities with His own disciples, the Bible also contains other relationships where the teaching and training of others occur. One prominent example is the association between Moses and Joshua.

When the Hebrew children fled Egyptian bondage, Joshua was an impressionable young man with outstanding qualities. His budding potential, with proper training and the Lord's blessing, could advance kingdom priorities. The Bible introduces Joshua as a field commander under Moses in Israel's battle against Amalek, a military engagement occurring shortly after the exodus. Even in this beginning episode, we see mentoring in progress (Ex. 17:8–16):

> Then Amalek came and fought against Israel at Rephidim. So Moses said to Joshua, "Choose men for us and go out, fight against Amalek. Tomorrow I will station myself on the top of the hill with the staff of God in my hand." Joshua did as Moses told him, and fought against Amalek; and Moses, Aaron, and Hur went up to the top of the hill. So it came about when Moses held his hand up, that Israel prevailed, and when he let his hand down, Amalek prevailed. But Moses' hands were heavy. Then they took a stone and put it under him, and he sat on it; and Aaron and Hur supported his hands, one on one side and one on the other. Thus his hands were steady until the sun set. So Joshua overwhelmed Amalek and his people with the edge of the sword. Then the LORD said to Moses, "Write this in a book as a memorial and recite it to Joshua, that I will utterly blot out the memory of Amalek from under heaven." Moses built an altar and named it The LORD is My Banner; and he said, "The LORD has sworn; the LORD will have war against Amalek from generation to generation."

The realm of military obligation is not outside the boundaries of Moses' guidance to Joshua. Moses trusts Joshua with Israel's army, and vulnerable military positions become opportunities for demonstrating truth. Moses mentors Joshua during military campaigns.

The responsibility of choosing fighting men in Exodus 17:9 is placed in the hands of Joshua as Moses says, "Choose men for us and go out, fight against Amalek." Just as Jesus entrusted His disciples with the lessons He taught them, so Moses trusts Joshua. This becomes a suitable testing ground for the young apprentice. Like any good mentor, Moses stands with his mentoree, allowing Joshua the victorious battlefield experience while he handles the staff of God. Moses assures his protégé that while Joshua is boldly engaging the enemy, he will participate by overseeing the Lord's staff. Even in this military encounter, we see the mentor and mentoree working together—one in the thick of battle and one handling the staff of God.

As Moses raises up his staff, another valuable lesson is learned. While his arms are in the air, the battle turns in Joshua's favor, but when Moses' arms are down, defeat looms. This places Joshua in quite a predicament. It matters little how strategic his battle skills are, or how large and brave his army appears. The deciding factor is whether Moses' arms are up or down. The victorious momentum is in the raised staff of God.

Joshua sees firsthand that victory and defeat are in the hands of the Lord. Human abilities, wisdom, skills, and might are no match for God's supernatural power. One day in the not-too-distant future, Moses will die and Joshua will take his place in leadership. Understanding that victory and success come from the hand of the Lord is a fundamental leadership lesson for Joshua to grasp.

The Lord may have had this very leadership lesson in mind as He instructs Moses to "write this in a book as a memorial" (Ex. 17:14) and directs Moses to "recite it to Joshua, that I will utterly blot out the memory of Amalek from under heaven" (Ex. 17:14). Modeling the proper response to God's remarkable battlefield victory, Moses builds an altar and names it "The Lord is My Banner" (Ex. 17:15).

Joshua is not only a great military leader, he is also a spiritual disciple of Moses. When Moses ascends Mt. Sinai to receive the sacred Ten Commandments, Joshua accompanies him part of the way to keep watch, as Exodus 24:13–18 indicates:

> So Moses arose with Joshua his servant, and Moses went up to the mountain of God. But to the elders he said, "Wait here for us until we return to you. And behold, Aaron and Hur are with you; whoever has a legal matter, let him approach them." Then Moses went up to the mountain, and the cloud covered the mountain. The glory of the Lord rested on Mount Sinai,

and the cloud covered it for six days; and on the seventh day He called to Moses from the midst of the cloud. And to the eyes of the sons of Israel the appearance of the glory of the Lord was like a consuming fire on the mountain top. Moses entered the midst of the cloud as he went up to the mountain; and Moses was on the mountain forty days and forty nights.

Moses' meeting with God on the mountain top is an historic event in the life of Israel. Take notice of who accompanies Moses—his servant Joshua. In speaking to the elders Moses says, "Wait here for *us* until *we* return to you" (Ex. 24:14). Mentor and mentoree climb the mountain together.

I wonder what they talked about during their joint endeavor? It is doubtful trivial matters were discussed such as, "Joshua, sure hope the weather holds up." It is more probable that Moses is teaching his mentoree. Though Joshua is restricted from traveling to the top with Moses, no one else even comes close to going as far as Joshua. This is a special privilege. As they walk the mountain together, Moses mentors Joshua. Surely Joshua ponders these things in his heart as he keeps watch over his esteemed mentor.

When Moses finally descends from the mountain top, Joshua is the first to warn him of the impending debacle down below: "Now when Joshua heard the sound of the people as they shouted, he said to Moses, 'There is a sound of war in the camp'" (Ex. 32:17). Though they were far from the camp, Moses discerns the sound of singing. Joshua is about to see the righteous anger of a holy man responding to a disgraceful golden calf incident. It must have come as a shock for Joshua to see the Hebrews so quickly turn against the God who had marvelously delivered the nation from the bonds of slavery. Moses not only displays anger toward their hideous offense, but his intercession actually spares their lives. We find another mentoring situation in the very next chapter. After the shameful golden calf incident we read these words in Exodus 33:1–11:

> Then the Lord spoke to Moses, "Depart, go up from here, you and the people whom you have brought up from the land of Egypt, to the land of which I swore to Abraham, Isaac, and Jacob, saying, 'To your descendants I will give it.' I will send an angel before you and I will drive out the Canaanite, the Amorite, the Hittite, the Perizzite, the Hivite and the

Jebusite. Go up to a land flowing with milk and honey; for I will not go up in your midst, because you are an obstinate people, and I might destroy you on the way."

When the people heard this sad word, they went into mourning, and none of them put on his ornaments. For the Lord had said to Moses, "Say to the sons of Israel, 'You are an obstinate people; should I go up in your midst for one moment, I would destroy you. Now therefore, put off your ornaments from you, that I may know what I shall do with you.'" So the sons of Israel stripped themselves of their ornaments, from Mount Horeb onward.

Now Moses used to take the tent and pitch it outside the camp, a good distance from the camp, and he called it the tent of meeting. And everyone who sought the Lord would go out to the tent of meeting which was outside the camp. And it came about, whenever Moses went out to the tent, that all the people would arise and stand, each at the entrance of his tent, and gaze after Moses until he entered the tent. Whenever Moses entered the tent, the pillar of cloud would descend and stand at the entrance of the tent; and the Lord would speak with Moses. When all the people saw the pillar of cloud standing at the entrance of the tent, all the people would arise and worship, each at the entrance of his tent. Thus the Lord used to speak to Moses face to face, just as a man speaks to his friend. When Moses returned to the camp, his servant Joshua, the son of Nun, a young man, would not depart from the tent.

Joshua's mentor happens to be the leader of a large traveling nation. Whether the Israelites move or stay depends on the Lord's instruction to Moses. Joshua watches this very carefully, realizing that Moses maintains a unique relationship with God. When Moses enters the tent, the Lord descends upon it in a pillar of cloud. Exodus 33:11 reflects this intimate relationship: "Thus, the Lord used to speak to Moses face to face, just as a man speaks to his friend." We all yearn for this kind of intimacy with God, and when Moses returns to camp, his mentoree refuses to depart from the tent.

Why would Joshua be unwilling to depart from the tent of meeting? As a military man, is it his duty to guard the tent? This seems highly unlikely since he is a high military official with others at his disposal. The context of the passage does not suggest this as the reason for his refusal to leave. He lingers at the tent of meeting, in my opinion, because he desires a similar relationship with God. He yearns for the intimacy with God that Moses experiences.

As an impressionable and passionate individual, Joshua needs to be harnessed, focused, and pointed in the right direction. He loves Moses dearly and is absorbing a great deal about spiritual leadership and maintaining a vital relationship with God. He is learning to lead, pray, and wait upon the Lord. Later in his life, after taking over for Moses, Joshua utilizes this knowledge of prayer and waiting on the Lord to lead the Israelites into the Promised Land.

On this particular occasion at the tent of meeting, it is quite possible that Joshua hears the compelling prayer of Moses in Exodus 33:13: "Now therefore, I pray You, if I have found favor in Your sight, let me know Your ways that I may know You, so that I may find favor in Your sight. Consider too, that this nation is Your people."

What an outstanding example for Joshua. After God informs the Israelites that they are an obstinate people and that He will not go with them, Moses intercedes on their behalf, realizing that moving into the Promised Land without God's presence will be devastating. He appeals to the endless compassion and mercy of the Lord. God acknowledges Moses' prayer and assures him in Exodus 33:14, "My presence shall go with you, and I will give you rest."

Walk in Moses' shoes for a moment. He could have easily thrown his hands in the air and declared, "That's it! I've had it up to here with you belly-achers." After all, they have given him nothing but trouble since the day they left Egypt. I wonder if Moses recalls the watchful eye of his mentoree taking note of his responses in tough situations. Keenly aware that Moses can dispense thoughtful advice, Joshua yearns to see if Moses actually lives what he says he believes. As God is preparing him for leadership, Joshua is observing Moses' example, in both word and deed.

Moses not only does what is right, but multiplies his own obedience by impacting his protégé. The words and actions of Moses play an integral role in molding and shaping Joshua for effective kingdom service. That is one of the things mentors do for their mentorees. Joshua possesses great respect for Moses, and yet, as great as Moses is, even he seeks to know God more intimately. With a mentor like Moses, we can't help but conclude that Joshua learns some valuable lessons that serve him well in the years after Moses' death.

In Numbers 11, the Hebrews are once again complaining, so Moses asks the Lord for help in carrying the heavy weight of responsibility. Moses is instructed to gather seventy elders to assist in shouldering the burden. Upon gathering the seventy elders, he stations them around the tent of meeting, and we read what happens next in Numbers 11:25–30:

> Then the LORD came down in the cloud and spoke to him; and He took of the Spirit who was upon him and placed Him upon the seventy elders. And when the Spirit rested upon them, they prophesied. But they did not do it again.
>
> But two men had remained in the camp; the name of one was Eldad and the name of the other Medad. And the Spirit rested upon them (now they were among those who had been registered, but had not gone out to the tent), and they prophesied in the camp. So a young man ran and told Moses and said, "Eldad and Medad are prophesying in the camp." Then Joshua the son of Nun, the attendant of Moses from his youth, said, "Moses, my lord, restrain them." But Moses said to him, "Are you jealous for my sake? Would that all the LORD's people were prophets, that the LORD would put His Spirit upon them!" Then Moses returned to the camp, both he and the elders of Israel.

This passage reveals Joshua's deep respect and love for his mentor. He sees firsthand how Moses speaks with God and leads the people. Moses deserves respect and honor from the congregation. In the mind of Joshua, Eldad and Medad's prophesying is a threat to his mentor, for they have not walked the arduous road Moses has traveled. They have not waited upon the Lord in the tent of meeting like Moses. They have not spoken face-to-face with the Lord like Moses. They were not chosen to lead like Moses. By prophesying, they are infringing upon the prerogatives of the revered leader—treading upon turf that does not rightfully belong to them. Recognizing Joshua's honest misjudgment, Moses gently corrects him. It is yet another situation where Moses models leadership, guidance, and vulnerability.

One key piece of evidence that Moses' mentoring takes root in Joshua's life is found in the account of the twelve spies reporting on their inspection of the Promised Land. Out of twelve spies, Joshua and Caleb are the only two who provide an encouraging report and exhort the people to trust God and move forward. Numbers 13:25–33 and 14:1–10 recount the story:

> When they returned from spying out the land, at the end of forty days, they proceeded to come to Moses and Aaron and to all the congregation of the sons of Israel in the wilderness of Paran, at Kadesh; and they brought back word to them and to all the congregation and showed them the fruit of the land. Thus they told him, and said, "We went in to the land where you sent us; and it certainly does flow with milk and honey, and this is its fruit. Nevertheless, the people who live in the land are strong, and the cities are fortified and very large; and moreover, we saw the descendants of Anak there. Amalek is living in the land of the Negev and the Hittites and the Jebusites and the Amorites are living in the hill country, and the Canaanites are living by the sea and by the side of the Jordan."
>
> Then Caleb quieted the people before Moses and said, "We should by all means go up and take possession of it, for we will surely overcome it." But the men who had gone up with him said, "We are not able to go up against the people, for they are too strong for us." So they gave out to the sons of Israel a bad report of the land which they had spied out, saying, "The land through which we have gone, in spying it out, is a land that devours its inhabitants; and all the people whom we saw in it are men of great size. There also we saw the Nephilim (the sons of Anak are part of the Nephilim); and we became like grasshoppers in our own sight, and so we were in their sight."
>
> Then all the congregation lifted up their voices and cried, and the people wept that night. All the sons of Israel grumbled against Moses and Aaron; and the whole congregation said to them, "Would that we had died in the land of Egypt! Or would that we had died in this wilderness! Why is the Lord bringing us into this land, to fall by the sword? Our wives and our little ones will become plunder; would it not be better for us to return to Egypt?" So they said to one another, "Let us appoint a leader and return to Egypt."

> Then Moses and Aaron fell on their faces in the presence of all the assembly of the congregation of the sons of Israel. Joshua the son of Nun and Caleb the son of Jephunneh, of those who had spied out the land, tore their clothes; and they spoke to all the congregation of the sons of Israel, saying, "The land which we passed through to spy out is an exceedingly good land. If the Lord is pleased with us, then He will bring us into this land and give it to us—a land which flows with milk and honey. Only do not rebel against the Lord; and do not fear the people of the land, for they will be our prey. Their protection has been removed from them, and the Lord is with us; do not fear them." But all the congregation said to stone them with stones. Then the glory of the Lord appeared in the tent of meeting to all the sons of Israel.

Fear often prevents us from obeying God, conquering promised lands, and progressing in the Spirit's leading. Fear is a major issue for the Hebrew nation, and it prevents them from doing what is right. Their destiny is to conquer the Promised Land and secure possession of what God has pledged. Yet, they focus on the negatives and forget the positives, like God's ability and power, His past performance, and His faithful promises. Despite Joshua and Caleb's advocacy for moving forward in faith, terror prevails in the camp.

It is difficult to imagine trepidation so great that it prompts their desire for a new leader and a return to Egyptian bondage rather than pursuing the faithful promises of God. Once again, we find the freed slaves grumbling and complaining, blaming God, doubting His sure leading, and envying past enslavement over present conditions. This is tantamount to slapping God in the face. At these horrific statements, Joshua tears his clothes and assures the congregation that the promised inheritance is a good land and its enemies will become prey instead of predators because the Lord has removed their protection (Num. 14:6–9). The inhabitants of the land are exposed and vulnerable without the protection of the Lord and unable to stand against the Hebrew nation. Despite Joshua's pleading, the former slaves rebel against the Lord.

These are insightful and mature words from the impressionable Joshua. In this volatile situation, he speaks wisely, confidently, and accurately. He exhibits firm confidence in God's ability. The years of mentoring influence under Moses pays off in this faith-testing moment. Moses models his teaching well.

This is one example that evidences the positive outcome of successful mentoring. It is time for Joshua to assert his faith in Yahweh and counteract the unbelieving and defeatist attitude of the Hebrew people. He does well.

It is quite remarkable to find Moses still mentoring Joshua during the transition of power and leadership. Despite Joshua's proven military record, spiritual leadership qualities, and mentoree status over the years, Moses will not choose him as a successor apart from divine selection. The transition of power and leadership is recorded in Numbers 27:15–23:

> Then Moses spoke to the LORD, saying, "May the LORD, the God of the spirits of all flesh, appoint a man over the congregation, who will go out and come in before them, and who will lead them out and bring them in, so that the congregation of the LORD will not be like sheep which have no shepherd." So the LORD said to Moses, "Take Joshua the son of Nun, a man in whom is the Spirit, and lay your hand on him; and have him stand before Eleazar the priest and before all the congregation, and commission him in their sight. You shall put some of your authority on him, in order that all the congregation of the sons of Israel may obey him. Moreover, he shall stand before Eleazar the priest, who shall inquire for him by the judgment of the Urim before the LORD. At his command they shall go out and at his command they shall come in, both he and the sons of Israel with him, even all the congregation." Moses did just as the LORD commanded him; and he took Joshua and set him before Eleazar the priest and before all the congregation. Then he laid his hands on him and commissioned him, just as the LORD had spoken through Moses.

This is payday for all the hard work Joshua puts in as a motivated mentoree. Obviously, not every apprentice is charged with this type of leadership role, but a time comes when mentorees are fully unleashed. For Joshua, the apprentice years under the gentle hand of Moses is worth its weight in gold. Joshua learns to pray, wait upon the Lord, and care for those he leads. Moses takes Joshua under his wings, tutors him in the ways of God, and models what he is trying to teach. As Jesus did with his disciples, so Moses does with Joshua. Moses places himself in vulnerable positions with his own people and enemy armies in order to demonstrate essential truths. He trusts Joshua with new learning and provides opportunity for success in various situations. This mentoring relationship trains Joshua to become the successor to Moses, the next leader of emerging Israel.

I wonder how Joshua and Moses might have reacted if God had selected someone other than Joshua to lead the nation? Both are strong in the Lord and understand that the choice is God's alone, and both are mature enough to leave the matter in God's hands. Had God selected someone else, Caleb for example, I believe both Moses and Joshua would have fully embraced the selection and pledged their unreserved support. It would have required a great amount of spiritual maturity to react in such a manner, but then again, isn't spiritual maturity one of the very reasons God selects Joshua?

There is an uncanny similarity between Joshua's tenure and that of Moses. Yahweh is with Joshua as He was with Moses (Josh. 1:5; 3:7). The people pledge to obey Joshua as they pledge to obey Moses (Josh. 1:17). Joshua sanctifies Israel as Moses does before Yahweh's miracles (Josh. 3:5; Ex. 19:14). The Lord promises to exalt Joshua as He exalted Moses (Josh. 3:7; 4:14). Both miraculously cross water, and in both instances the waters stand in a heap while the tribes of Israel cross on dry ground (Josh. 3:17; Ex. 14:21–23, 29). At the outset of his mission to conquer the Promised Land, Joshua encounters the commander of Yahweh's army and is told, as was Moses (Josh 5:15; Ex. 3:5), "Remove your sandals from your feet, for the place where you are standing is holy." Both Moses and Joshua intercede for an errant congregation (Josh. 7:7; Dt. 9:25–29). Both write the law on stones (Josh. 8:32), and Yahweh hardens the hearts of their enemies (Josh. 11:20; Ex. 9:12).

At the end of their life's work, both Moses and Joshua deliver stirring messages of appeal and warning to the assembled Israelites and both men die at symbolic ages (Moses 120 and Joshua 110), having reached what was considered the ideal Egyptian lifespan (110). The similarity of their lives is a strong indication of the impact of mentoring.

ELIJAH AND ELISHA

In addition to the biblical example of Moses and Joshua, another inspiring mentoring relationship involves Elijah and Elisha. The characters and circumstances are quite different from that of Moses and Joshua. While Moses and Joshua escape Egypt and conquer the Promised Land, Elijah and Elisha minister in the ninth century to an already established nation that has fallen from their previous spiritual position. Moses and Joshua are similar in character, but Elijah and Elisha are remarkably different. Elijah is a true Bedouin child of the desert, while Elisha prefers the hustle and bustle of city life. Elijah favors solitude, while Elisha desires companionship.

Though Elisha continues the work of Elijah, his calling takes on a new dimension not seen in Elijah's ministry. Elijah plays the role of accuser, while Elisha plays the role of healer. Elijah's ministry involves publicly exposing sin and proclaiming judgment, while Elisha brings miracles and healing. Elisha restores life where there is death, increases the widow's oil resources, makes bitter waters pure, offers tender sympathy for friends, and sheds tears of sorrow for the predicament of his country.

It is clear from these stark contrasts that there is plenty of room for diversity between mentor and mentoree. Mentoring relationships can be highly successful even when significant differences exist. Exact cloning is not essential, nor is it desired. The point of mentoring is not to make someone exactly like you, but to empower others through the sharing of God-given resources to become the very best they can be. Elijah and Elisha establish a mentoring relationship even though there are vast differences between them.

Elisha's association with Elijah begins shortly after the confrontation between Elijah and Ahab on Mt. Carmel. Elisha is plowing his father's fields when the divine call arrives. Without a word, Elijah, on his way from Mt. Horeb to Damascus, throws his mantle upon Elisha's shoulder, a token of investiture to the prophet's office and of adoption as a son. Elisha understands the significance of this gesture and pledges himself immediately. His resolve to serve is seen in the formal leave he takes from his family. From now on he becomes a devoted servant to Elijah and Elijah's God. The beginning of the mentoring relationship occurs in I Kings 19:15–21:

> The Lord said to him, "Go, return on your way to the wilderness of Damascus, and when you have arrived, you shall anoint Hazael king over Aram; and Jehu the son of Nimshi you shall anoint king over Israel; and Elisha the son of Shaphat of Abel-meholah you shall anoint as prophet in your place. It shall come about, the one who escapes from the sword of Hazael, Jehu shall put to death, and the one who escapes from the sword

> of Jehu, Elisha shall put to death. Yet I will leave 7,000 in Israel, all the knees that have not bowed to Baal and every mouth that has not kissed him."
>
> So he departed from there and found Elisha the son of Shaphat, while he was plowing with twelve pairs of oxen before him, and he with the twelfth. And Elijah passed over to him and threw his mantle on him. He left the oxen and ran after Elijah and said, "Please let me kiss my father and my mother, then I will follow you." And he said to him, "Go back again, for what have I done to you?" So he returned from following him, and took the pair of oxen and sacrificed them and boiled their flesh with the implements of the oxen, and gave it to the people and they ate. Then he arose and followed Elijah and ministered to him.

Elijah is divinely informed of his mentoring assignment and accepts that Elisha is to be his prophetic replacement, so before anointing Hazael and Jehu as kings, he first calls Elisha. If Elisha is going to be a prophet, he must enter his training right away. By procuring Elisha first, Elijah provides a teachable moment that will further Elisha's prophetic training. Elisha also realizes that an apprenticeship is about to begin that will forever change his life—from plowing fields to the prophetic ministry.

After the mentoring relationship is established, we do not hear much about Elisha until he accompanies Elijah to the other side of the Jordan and witnesses Elijah's magnificent ascension. Elisha perceives that it is time for Yahweh to call Elijah home, as 2 Kings 2:3–5 states:

> Then the sons of the prophets who were at Bethel came out to Elisha and said to him, "Do you know that the Lord will take away your master from over you today?" And he said, "Yes, I know; be still." Elijah said to him, "Elisha, please stay here, for the Lord has sent me to Jericho." But he said, "As the Lord lives, and as you yourself live, I will not leave you." So they came to Jericho. The sons of the prophets who were at Jericho approached Elisha and said to him, "Do you know that the Lord will take away your master from over you today?" And he answered, "Yes, I know; be still."

After spending several years under Elijah's wings, Elisha realizes that it is now time for his mentor to depart and for him to assume the prophetic office.

His term of apprenticeship under Elijah must have been meaningful, for on three occasions Elijah offers to release him from the responsibility of the prophetic office and Elisha declines. At Gilgal (2 Kgs.2:2), Elijah says, "Stay here please, for the Lord has sent me as far as Bethel." But Elisha responds, "As the Lord lives and as you yourself live, I will not leave you." While in Jericho, Elijah offers to release Elisha one final time (2 Kgs. 2:6) by saying, "Please stay here, for the Lord has sent me to the Jordan." With steadfast resolve, Elisha vehemently refuses by answering, "As the Lord lives, and as you yourself live, I will not leave you."

Had Elisha not learned a thing from Elijah, had the mentoring relationship not been meaningful, had it merely been a waste of several years, and had he wanted to go back to farming, Elisha surely would have accepted Elijah's release. In reality, the mentoring relationship has prepared him for this time of testing. He knows beyond a shadow of a doubt what the Lord desires and that his apprenticeship under Elijah's tutelage makes him a better prophet. Because God divinely leads Elisha into a mentoring relationship with the honorable prophet, he is prepared to assume the burdens and responsibilities of the office upon Elijah's departure.

Realizing that his departure is imminent and that Elisha remains faithful to his call, Elijah asks Elisha what he can do for him before he is taken away. Elisha's wise answer speaks positively of his time under Elijah's mentorship. Realizing that the prophetic ministry is no easy task and without God's blessing he will fail, Elisha asks for a double portion of Elijah's spirit as seen in 2 Kings 2:9–14:

> When they had crossed over, Elijah said to Elisha, "Ask what I shall do for you before I am taken from you." And Elisha said, "Please, let a double portion of your spirit be upon me." He said, "You have asked a hard thing. Nevertheless, if you see me when I am taken from you, it shall be so for you; but if not, it shall not be so." As they were going along and talking, behold, there appeared a chariot of fire and horses of fire which separated the two of them. And Elijah went up by a whirlwind to heaven. Elisha saw it and cried out, "My father, my father, the chariots of Israel and its horsemen!" And he saw Elijah no more. Then he took hold of his own clothes and tore them in two pieces. He also took up the mantle of Elijah

that fell from him and returned and stood by the bank of the Jordan. He took the mantle of Elijah that fell from him and struck the waters and said, "Where is the Lord, the God of Elijah?" And when he also had struck the waters, they were divided here and there; and Elisha crossed over.

Elisha *did* see Elijah taken from him and was given a double portion of his spirit. For the next fifty years, Elisha continues his ministry in the northern kingdom—a ministry accompanied by impressive miracles that reflect the double portion of the spirit given to him.

Though not much is said regarding their mentoring bond, the end result informs us of what the relationship must have been like. In 2 Kings 2:12, Elisha tenderly calls Elijah, "my father, my father." Elisha's refusal to accept the offered release from ministry and his wise request for a double portion of Elijah's spirit speaks to the impact of the apprenticeship. Elijah models the prophetic office for Elisha. Together they encounter situations requiring wisdom and guidance from the Lord. Elisha keenly picks up what is taught and modeled for him, succeeds Elijah, and begins his own powerful prophetic ministry.

These are just two of the many mentoring scenarios found in the Old Testament. In turning to the New Testament, we find similar examples of mentoring's powerful influence.

PAUL AND TIMOTHY

During Paul's second missionary journey, he stops in Derbe and Lystra, two cities located in south-central Asia Minor. Here he meets young Timothy, who is first mentioned in Acts 16:1–2: "Paul came also to Derbe and to Lystra. And a disciple was there, named Timothy, the son of a Jewish woman who was a believer, but his father was a Greek, and he was well spoken of by the brethren who were in Lystra and Iconium." The term "disciple" (*mathetes*) indicates that Timothy is a believer. His mother is Jewish, while his father is a Gentile.

Paul affectionately considers Timothy his spiritual child in the faith. In 1 Corinthians 4:17, Paul calls Timothy "my beloved and faithful child in the Lord," while in 1 Timothy 1:2, Paul refers to him as "my true child in the faith." Exactly how Timothy comes to faith is not revealed in Scripture. It is quite possible that Paul, Timothy's spiritual father, was directly responsible for his conversion.

Timothy also possesses a heritage of faith that first resided in his grandmother Lois and then in his mother Eunice. Even if Timothy became a Christian through the influence of his mother and grandmother, it is conceivable that they first heard the gospel through Paul's missionary endeavors to the region. Since Paul is either directly or indirectly responsible for Timothy's conversion and the two of them maintain such a close working relationship, Paul can easily justify calling Timothy "my true child in the faith." Their mentoring relationship begins with Timothy's conversion. In due time, Paul places Timothy under his wings, brings him along on ministry journeys (Acts 16:3), and assigns him special duties and responsibilities.

On several occasions, Paul leaves Timothy behind so that he might accomplish a particular task. Good mentors are not afraid to place appropriate responsibility in the hands of those they mentor. On one occasion, as noted in Acts 17:13–15, Timothy remains to encourage persecuted Christians and serve as a decoy so Paul can bypass the aggressive Jews of Thessalonica:

> But when the Jews of Thessalonica found out that the word of God had been proclaimed by Paul in Berea also, they came there as well, agitating and stirring up the crowds. Then immediately the brethren sent Paul out to go as far as the sea; and Silas and Timothy remained there. Now those who escorted Paul brought him as far as Athens; and receiving a command for Silas and Timothy to come to him as soon as possible, they left.

On other occasions, Paul employs Timothy as an emissary to do what he himself cannot do. For instance, as the Macedonian Christians endure persecution, Paul sends Timothy to Thessalonica so their faith might be strengthened. 1 Thessalonians 3:1–3 says,

> Therefore when we could endure it no longer, we thought it best to be left behind at Athens alone, and we sent Timothy, our brother and God's fellow worker in the gospel of Christ, to strengthen and encourage you as to your faith, so that no one would be disturbed by these afflictions; for you yourselves know that we have been destined for this.

Later in Acts 19:22, Paul sends Timothy out from Ephesus to other Macedonian churches, perhaps with the same objective. After each mission, Timothy rejoins Paul as soon as possible. Coming together after an assignment is the perfect time for Timothy to report on the special mission Paul entrusts to him. It is also a wonderful opportunity for regaining perspective, receiving helpful advice, and cherishing encouragement and assessment from Paul, his treasured mentor.

Timothy is also associated with Paul's ministry in Ephesus and Corinth, and he travels with him on the journey to Jerusalem, as noted in Acts 20:4–5. When Paul is released from prison and engages in further ministry activities to the east, he leaves Timothy behind at Ephesus. Later, in Hebrews 13:23, Timothy himself becomes a prisoner, although no details of his imprisonment are revealed. Surely, his perspective and behavior while in prison are modeled after Paul, who himself experienced prison life and exemplified appropriate and godly responses during times of forced confinement.

Upon Timothy's conversion, Paul takes him under his wing, brings him along on missionary journeys, and designates special tasks and responsibilities that test the practical application of his new learning. Paul must have experienced intense joy as he watched his "true child in the faith" grow, mature, and make significant contributions to the lives of others. In Philippians 2:20–22, Paul proudly commends Timothy to the church in Philippi:

> For I have no one else of kindred spirit who will genuinely be concerned for your welfare. For they all seek after their own interests, not those of Christ Jesus. But you know of his proven worth, that he served with me in the furtherance of the gospel like a child serving his father.

Paul finds exceptional comfort and strength from his relationship with Timothy. Mentoring can be two-sided. It is not one person draining time and energy from another person. The relationship should be mutually beneficial. Mentors find themselves in powerful positions of influence as they pour their work, knowledge, gifts, skills, and experiences into others. Mentors, in a sense, multiply their own work and efforts by investing in others. Without a doubt,

Paul's spiritual harvest is furthered by his investment in Timothy's life. Long after Paul's last breath, Timothy's ministry remains. Mentoring relationships can be positive, rewarding, and productive for all involved.

Just as Silas took Barnabas' place as Paul's senior associate on his second missionary journey in Acts 15:26–41, so Timothy replaces Mark as Paul's junior associate. As Paul invests time and energy into the relationship, Timothy proves to be the type of protégé a mentor hopes to find. He dedicates himself to new learning and devotes himself wholeheartedly to ministry. In doing so, he becomes Paul's valuable friend and trusted colleague.

Paul's deep affection for young Timothy can be seen in his references to him as "my fellow worker" in Romans 16:21, and "God's fellow worker" in I Thessalonians 3:2. Paul reveals, in 2 Timothy 1:3, that Timothy is constantly in his prayers both night and day. Paul longs to see his spiritual son and recalls him with tender tears (2 Tim. 1:4).

Realizing that Timothy is a young apprentice in the faith, Paul is even willing to admonish him. For instance, Timothy was at one time a timid individual, so Paul cautions him in 2 Timothy 1:7, "For God has not given us a spirit of timidity, but of power and love and discipline." In 2 Timothy 1:8, Paul encourages Timothy not to be ashamed of the testimony of the Lord or his association with Paul, but to join him in suffering for the Lord's sake. 2 Timothy 1:2–8 is worth reading:

> To Timothy, my beloved son: Grace, mercy and peace from God the Father and Christ Jesus our Lord. I thank God, whom I serve with a clear conscience the way my forefathers did, as I constantly remember you in my prayers night and day, longing to see you, even as I recall your tears, so that I may be filled with joy. For I am mindful of the sincere faith within you, which first dwelt in your grandmother Lois and your mother Eunice, and I am sure that it is in you as well. For this reason I remind you to kindle afresh the gift of God which is in you through the laying on of my hands. For God has not given us a spirit of timidity, but of power and love and discipline. Therefore do not be ashamed of the testimony of our Lord or of me His prisoner, but join with me in suffering for the gospel according to the power of God.

Affectionate phrases and encouraging words, as well as Paul's admonitions to his young protégé, fill the pages of 2 Timothy. The apprentice is admonished to remain strong in the Lord's grace and continue being a good soldier in God's army (2 Tim. 2:1–7). Paul admonishes Timothy to be an unashamed workman for the Lord in 2 Timothy 2:15–16:

> Be diligent to present yourself approved to God as a workman who does not need to be ashamed, accurately handling the word of truth. But avoid worldly and empty chatter, for it will lead to further ungodliness.

Paul reminds his spiritual son to flee from youthful lusts and pursue righteousness: "Now flee from youthful lusts and pursue righteousness, faith, love and peace, with those who call on the Lord from a pure heart" (2 Tim 2:22). He further warns him of difficult times to come: "But realize this, that in the last days difficult times will come" (2 Tim. 3:1). Timothy is challenged to continue preaching in 2 Timothy 4:1, and in closing his letter, Paul beseeches Timothy to "make every effort to come to me soon" (2 Tim. 4:9).

It is easy to see from the preceding scriptural examples that mentoring is a biblical process. Jesus mentors His disciples, and they change the world. Moses mentors Joshua, and the Promised Land is conquered and an inheritance claimed. Elijah mentors Elisha, and a double portion of his spirit falls upon Elisha as he continues the difficult tasks associated with his prophetic call. He maintains a powerful ministry in the northern kingdom for the next fifty years. Paul mentors his beloved Timothy who becomes a workman of God, unashamed of the gospel, and accurately handles the task of preaching. Not everyone will soar to the same heights, but the impact of mentoring can be just as meaningful.

Mentoring, as we have defined it, is a relational experience in which one person empowers another by sharing God-given resources. Scriptural examples put flesh and bones to this definition. Each mentoring scenario occurs in the context of relationship, with one individual (mentor) sharing God-given resources with another individual (mentoree). The end result is empowerment. Timothy becomes a better pastor. Elisha becomes a powerful prophet. Joshua replaces Moses as the leader of the Hebrew nation. Even the disciples are transformed by their relationship with Jesus and respond by spreading the gospel.

5

THE ACCOUNTABILITY FACTOR

ACCOUNTABILITY AND MENTORING

A critical ingredient in successful mentoring relationships is the accountability factor. Without it, mentoring is like baseball without hot dogs, marriage without love, a sermon without a congregation. It is hard to imagine one without the other.

On a recent vacation, our family attended a Minnesota Twins baseball game. We engaged in the tradition of eating a ballpark hot dog, an expensive adventure for our family. Since we rarely experience these events, we knew that without a hot dog, our baseball outing would be less than complete.

Similarly, mentoring without some degree of accountability is almost always less than complete. The greater the commitment and accountability one has to the mentoring relationship, the better chance of impact and empowerment for the participants.

Accountability Begins in the Mind

As with most things in life, our willingness to be accountable begins with a conscious decision to do so. A child, after being told by her parents to sit down, may be thinking to herself, "I may be sitting down on the outside, but I'm standing on the inside." Her inner defiance betrays her true feelings about the situation.

Our mind is the trigger point, or control room, for our behavior. Actions first begin as thoughts. This is why the Bible admonishes us to guard our thoughts, renew our minds, and think on those things which are of God. If people *want* to be accountable, they will be, since folks tend to do what they want to do.

Most individuals have little difficulty with the notion of being accountable to God. Yet, if a minister or elder board called the actions of a fellow Christian into account, they would likely hear something like this: "Well, who do you think you are? I don't have to account to you for one thing. I'll answer to God and God alone." In this particular case, an appeal to God is merely a front for selfish behavior and illustrates that people have no problem with the notion of answering to God (in theory anyway). One of the reasons they flippantly say this is because they are not standing before His majestic throne. They appeal to the Creator, knowing that He is not descending from the clouds to stand right in front of them and say, "Now, what were you saying?"

Sensible Christians, however, truly *do* understand the concept of answering to their Creator. They realize that although He is not physically in front of them, He is still present and hears their words, observes their behavior, and knows all they do and think. Hebrews 4:13 reminds us, "And there is no creature hidden from His sight, but all things are open and laid bare to the eyes of Him with whom we have to do." To understand something intellectually is quite different than allowing that understanding to influence how we live.

There are numerous biblical passages that speak of God knowing and seeing all things. Not only does He see, hear, and know all things, but He is said to maintain accurate accounts. In light of this, most Christians would agree with Romans 14:12, which says, "So then each one of us will give an account of himself to God." Since He alone is God, the perfect creator and sustainer of life, He has the right to judge our thoughts and actions. The prerogative is His alone.

The problem we have with accountability is not that we will someday be accountable to God, for we accept this as a theological truth that occurs in the distant future. It is not very real to us in this present life because God is not physically at hand to remind us of this inevitable accounting event. It is when the concept is brought down into the personal realm of everyday choices that resistance rears its ugly head. We hate having to be accountable to another human being, someone who will actually, in this life, hold us accountable for what we say and do. It is much easier, and often appears more spiritual, to appeal to our accountability with God, knowing full well that He is not inspecting our life in a tangible and physical manner right before us. Appealing to the accountability of God alone is merely camouflage that allows us to do as we please while justifying our actions under a religious cloak. It gives the impression that we are humbly obeying God, when in reality, the "accountability to God alone" phrase becomes a strategic devise to do as we please. Accountability is fine if the person on the rung below is accountable to us. It is when *we* have to be accountable to another person that problems arise and resistance roots down deep.

Accountability in America

America may be the best and worst place at the same time to maintain accountable relationships. It is the best place because we live in a free nation. There are no laws discouraging mentoring relationships, no totalitarian government restricting mentoring activities, or any genuine obstacles preventing us from being accountable to one another. In this prosperous country with its high standard of living, we are free to pursue accountable relationships to our heart's content. Mentoring relationships can blossom in America.

On the other hand, America may be one of the worst places for accountable relationships because of the prevalent individualistic nature of our society. It is not uncommon to come home from work, shut ourselves in our houses, and watch the tube all night while fiddling with some new social media outlet or technological device. One day, while driving through a popular subdivision, it struck me that the most visible aspect of this neighborhood was the massive garages facing the street. Every house in the subdivision had a three-car garage staring back at you as the most prominent aspect of its architecture. These homes were obviously built for seclusion—erected as barriers between neighbors. Pull quickly into the garage, shut the door, and you can retreat to a world of tranquility devoid of others. Within the peaceful seclusion of their home, owners can enjoy distance and safety from the entanglement of neighbors.

I confess, after spending many years on the frontline of kingdom ministry, that the scarcity of accountability and the surplus of selfish ambition reigning in the contemporary church alarms me. I receive numerous unsolicited stories from individuals sharing their dismal experience with insufficient accountability and selfish excesses in their local church. Their stories are sad and horrifying at the same time.

While I wish I could cast these scenarios off as mere anomalies in an otherwise tranquil church, the very opposite is true. Without the confines of accountability, destructive conflict sweeps across congregations like a runaway river, destroying everything in its path. Studies have confirmed what we have long suspected: most conflict in churches does not revolve around theological or moral concerns but is rooted in personality differences and personal preference issues. The individualistic "I" has uprooted the collective "we." When this occurs, accountability is thrown out the window. In an attempt to soothe the cognitive dissonance experienced in conflict, we often rationalize that accountability is for "her," never "me." It becomes an expectation of others, not of ourselves.

There are certain subjects that can be preached and taught, such as submission and accountability, and members of the congregation will nod their heads in collective assent. How can they not? One doesn't have to be a rocket scientist to find this gem of truth in Scripture. They *doctrinally* agree with the teaching. Intellectual assent, however, is much different than practical application! Ask the members of your local congregation to *actually practice* submission and accountability, and you might as well be racing a two-humped camel in the Indy 500.

My point is this: we have no problem stating that we are accountable to God and believing that accountability and submission are doctrinally correct things to do. The difficulty arises when we apply this doctrine to our own lives. Accountability, as doctrinally sound as it might be, simply does not agree with our taste buds.

Accountability is All Around Us

Accountability is not really a complicated concept to grasp in light of the fact that we see it all around us in the secular world. Institutions employ accountability on a regular and systematic basis; it is commonplace. A banker, for instance, holds clients accountable for car loans. Academic institutions hold students accountable to complete the necessary requirements for graduation. Employers hold employees accountable to performance standards. National governments hold their citizens responsible for obeying the laws of the land. We think nothing of these accountability structures. To do away with accountability would be nonsensical. Accountability is healthy and profitable for all involved. When there is no accountability, chaos emerges.

The twelve disciples were accountable to Jesus. Jesus Himself is accountable to the Father. Paul and Silas are accountable to the church in Antioch. Timothy is accountable to Paul. Onesimus, a slave, is accountable to his master. When David commits adultery with Bathsheba and murders Uriah, her husband, Nathan the prophet stands before the king and holds him accountable. Joseph is accountable to Potiphar. Saul is accountable to Samuel. Accountability is not only found in the secular world, but it is also a biblical concept portrayed in a positive light.

The most difficult aspect of accountability is not accepting that it is right, good, or doctrinally sound. The hardest aspect of accountability is personal acceptance—our willingness to be accountable to another. Accountability is good, yes, but it is not good for *me!* One significant reason for this aversion to personal acceptance is our inability to "slide by." When someone holds us accountable for our words, thoughts, and deeds, it becomes more difficult to get away with things—to slide by. Without accountability there is no watchful eye, no human voice scrutinizing our internal motivations and external actions, and no searchlight of the Holy Spirit exposing darkness in our heart. When accountability enters the picture, we must be diligent about our walk with God. No longer will we be able to fool those on the outside while ignoring those internal areas requiring attention.

During my college days, I picked my friend up at 5:30 a.m. and drove to the YMCA gym. Together, we sleepily endured the workout while yearning for one more hour under warm sheets. Things were different after we showered and got on with our day. We were glad to have exchanged one hour of sleep for a vigorous workout. It wasn't easy to haul ourselves out of bed in the middle of winter, but we did it. We did it because we had each other. We were accountable to one another. Try a workout on your own at 5:30 a.m., and you will quickly find yourself under soft sheets instead of heavy dumbbells.

Accountability doesn't allow us to remain in the comfort of our bed. It forces us toward the workout room, where we must become acquainted with being uncomfortable. Accountability is a God-given route to becoming more like our Lord. It keeps us true, sharpens us, and makes us better individuals for the kingdom. This is, of course, our goal. Isn't it? We want to be more like Jesus in thought, word, and deed. Jesus never promised that serving Him would be a piece of cake or a land of luxury. Nothing truly worthwhile is. I heard someone once say, "There is no growth in the comfort zone, and there is no comfort in the growth zone." The pursuit of accountability is wholly worthwhile. Mentoring relationships provide rewarding environments for accountability to blossom.

Accountability is not only for mentorees; it is to be modeled by mentors as well. If mentors desire the accountability of mentorees, they must model accountability themselves. Accountability is especially important in the areas of confidentiality and correction. Seasoned mentors do not pry for unnecessary details to broadcast as juicy gossip. That which *is* shared, is held in confidence. Mentors are not "untouchables" sitting in ivory towers as perfect individuals. By responding quickly to reproof in their own life, they set an example to others. All are subject to scriptural teaching, whether we are mentors or mentorees.

Wisdom from above is needed to provide appropriate accountability for mentorees. An objective opinion may be all that is needed, while some situations require more difficult conversations. At times, just being a sounding board is all it takes, while other circumstances demand straight talk. It is not an easy thing to be accountable to another person. In many respects, it is even more difficult to be the one to whom others are accountable. Exactly how accountability works itself out in mentoring relationships will largely be a combination of the mentoree's receptivity and the mentor's prayers, wisdom, experience, and guidance from God's Spirit.

INSPECTION VS. EXPECTATION

While serving as a full-time minister in the local church, I utilized a leadership program requiring extensive coursework, Scripture memorization, small group meetings, and objective testing. Quite successful, it was based on the simple premise that people tend to do what we *inspect*, not what we *expect*. Thus, we inspected and monitored weekly assignments and progress throughout the program. This laid the foundation for accountability, which in turn led to greater learning and stronger leaders. People do what we inspect, not necessarily what we expect.

There are several individuals in my life to whom I am accountable. I give them permission to say anything to me, call me on the carpet when necessary, and observe and comment on my life in order to make me a better servant of the Lord. As you might imagine, this is not always easy. Sometimes I don't like what they say, but I always know they have my best interest at heart.

Often I initiate the dialogue by sharing an incident with them and asking, "What do you think? Am I seeing things correctly? Is my behavior in line with biblical precepts?" When a positive response is generated, I feel encouraged and strengthened with a renewed commitment to right attitude and behavior. If the response is negative, I rethink the issue and attempt to alter my outlook and behaviors.

There are not many people in my life with whom I can be so open and trusting. We don't need a million people to hold us accountable; a few trusted individuals will do the trick. I absolutely love these honest, open, and accountable relationships. Please do not misunderstand; what they say isn't always easy to swallow, and sometimes it feels like a Volkswagen thrust down my throat. Because of the strong relationship, however, I know that it is just as difficult for them to say necessary words to me as it is for me to receive them.

Swallowing a Volkswagen is much easier when you know beyond a shadow of doubt that your mentors love you dearly and affirm your best interest and God's glory as their primary concern. Truth must always be accompanied by love (Eph. 4:15). Accountability without love is nothing more than shallow self-interest at the expense of another.

SPECIAL NOTE TO PASTORS

Regarding accountability, a special note must be conveyed to pastors that may be difficult for parishioners to fully understand. My comments arise from many years of firsthand experience in full-time ministry and are further backed by years of seminary and university teaching while interacting with pastors from various denominations on a regular basis.

Pastors are typically elevated to a pedestal of perceived perfection. Viewed as "having arrived" to some superhuman level of spirituality, they are often held to unrealistic expectations prescribed by individual members of the congregation. What I am about to say does not in any way diminish the fact that pastors, like everyone else, are accountable to God and the organizational hierarchy of their denomination.

There will always be, however, certain overzealous and misguided individuals who desire for pastors, and the rest of the world, to be accountable to them for everything. If pastors do not succumb to prescribed expectations, these individuals can make life miserable for them under the guise of Christian accountability. This is simply not right. Their "accountability" is nothing more than unfounded criticism and a desire to make others just like them. It is a control issue and has no place in the kingdom. *Not everyone has the right to be your mentor.* With the lofty expectations placed on ministers these days, the last thing they need is one more person using "accountability" as a mechanism for control, criticism, and condemnation.

I've seen it hundreds of times—churches scratching their heads and saying, "They just don't make pastors like they used to." Bending under the unrealistic expectations placed upon them, pastors are scratching their own heads and saying, "They sure don't make churches like they used to."

My point is this: if you are in a relationship that criticizes instead of encourages, that drains instead of strengthens, where you are asked to conform to another's picky minutia instead of character development, then you have the wrong mentor. These critical individuals have not garnered the right to hold you accountable because they do not have your best interest in mind.

Accountability always has in mind the best interest of the one who is accountable. When people use "accountability" to further their selfish agendas and personal ambitions, they have confused accountability with sin. To them, accountability is nothing more than a manipulative scheme for controlling others—a euphemism for using people. While this situation can happen to anyone, pastors are especially prone to such abuse because they are expected to be "all things to all people," an impossible standard to achieve.

When I found myself in such "accountable" relationships, I experienced severe exhaustion from always trying to measure up. I was nothing more than a hamster running endlessly on the play wheel, expending enormous amounts of energy but going nowhere. My self-appointed mentors cared very little for me personally. They were, however, extremely interested in using me to further their own ambitions.

Thank God not all mentors are the self-appointed and self-absorbed type. Life was breathed into my weary spirit when I found people who truly loved and cared for me, whose only agenda was my best interest and God's glory. Their words brought life rather than death, encouragement rather than discouragement. They re-energized my spirit and helped me yearn for personal change and growth. I was motivated to be more like Jesus because my mentors were safe and trustworthy.

When I refer to accountability, please understand that I am referring to accountability from those who have earned the right to be your mentor. I am referring to safe and trusted individuals who have your best interest at heart.

Proverbs contains numerous pearls of wisdom regarding trusting and safe relationships, such as the following:

Proverbs 13:10
But wisdom is with those who receive counsel.

Proverbs 13:14
The teaching of the wise is a fountain of life, to turn aside from the snares of death.

Proverbs 13:20
He who walks with wise men will be wise, but the companion of fools will suffer harm.

Proverbs 15:31
He whose ear listens to the life-giving reproof will dwell among the wise.

Proverbs 20:5
A plan in the heart of a man is like deep water, but a man of understanding draws it out.

Proverbs 24:26
He kisses the lips who gives a right answer.

Proverbs 27:17
Iron sharpens iron, so one man sharpens another.

Ecclesiastes 4:9–10
Two are better than one because they have a good return for their labor. For if either of them falls, the one will lift up his companion. But woe to the one who falls when there is not another to lift him up.

To the surprise of many, Proverbs 15:31 enlightens us to the fact that reproof *can* be life-giving. Unfortunately, much of the reproof we experience these days is anything but life-giving. Usually it is administered in near fatal doses and activates a chronic cycle of shame and anxiety. Yet, I have personally experienced reproof that is life-giving. Though the words were difficult to accept, I soaked them up like a sponge. In a twist of irony, words that could have maimed and destroyed became a refreshing balm that brought healing. Harsh words can become life-giving when they come from the lips of a safe and trusted individual who has our best interest in mind.

In Plato's *Dialogues*, (Apology, section 38), Socrates remarks that an unexamined life is not worth living. Even Jesus invites us to take the log out of our own eye before attempting to snatch the speck out of another person's eye (Mt. 7:1–5). Before beginning the solemn act of church discipline, Scripture exhorts us to first examine ourselves before discussing the trespass of another (Gal. 6:1).

The concept of self-examination is a biblical and necessary ingredient for spiritual maturity. The key is to find individuals who will help you do this in love. Don't allow just anyone to climb into your lap, point a long skinny finger at your nose, and rebuke you for not measuring up to *their* own agenda or personal preference. Find someone who loves to love you and who has earned the right of accountability.

Shortly after moving into the parsonage of a new pastorate, an attorney who attended the church stopped over, pulled me aside and said, "I was listening to Chuck Swindoll on the radio today and he said that we all need someone with whom we can be accountable. I don't have anyone like that in my life. Would you be willing to establish that kind of relationship with me?" Wow! Thank you, Chuck! I wish we had more people in our churches like this man, perceptive enough to recognize his need and courageous enough to initiate the mentoring relationship.

I am forever grateful to God for this man's influence upon my life. We held one another accountable because we intentionally created a safe environment for open and honest communication. We trusted each other, and when trust is established, we more readily climb out on a limb of risk, open up, and expose faults while experiencing love and acceptance from someone who sees our potential *and* our shortcomings. Never once was that trust violated. We not only held each other accountable for the big things in our spiritual life—such as prayer, Bible study, and right living—but we also held each other accountable for the little things as well.

One day, my trusted friend informed me that I had been unintentionally saying "wifes" instead of "wives" in my message series, so I made certain in the remaining messages to carefully enunciate for the benefit of the hearer. I corrected my grammar, and now I more carefully monitor how my public speech is perceived. It was a little thing, but he knew me well enough to know that I would appreciate his keen observation. He was not attempting to be nit-picky; he was only trying to help. Often, the intent and spirit of the mentor makes all the difference in the world as to whether a word is accepted or rejected.

On one occasion, I privately spoke with him about his children's behavior during church services. Do you realize what a touchy subject this is for most parents? He agreed with my observations, I gained greater understanding of his challenges, and there were no more problems. Accountability is a wonderful experience within the confines of a trusting, loving environment.

6

INFLUENCING OTHERS

BARNABAS, TIMOTHY, AND EPAPHRADITUS

In his book *The Fine Art of Mentoring*, Ted Engstrom writes, "Every Christian mentor needs a Barnabas to receive encouragement, a Timothy to guide as a protégé, and an Epaphraditus to enjoy on a peer level." [9]

Barnabas represents those who provide constant encouragement—something we could all use more of in our lives! He is a big-hearted fellow who always sees the potential in others. For instance, when the rest of the church seeks to keep its distance from Paul after his conversion, Barnabas befriends him. While his colleagues in ministry remember Paul as the malicious one who persecutes Christians with relentless zeal, Barnabas sees him as a new convert with potential for kingdom impact. He recognizes God's handiwork in Paul's life. This is not, as some may have proposed, some twisted plan of Paul's to infiltrate and murder more Christians.

So that Paul could share his testimony, we discover in Acts 9:27 that "Barnabas took hold of him and brought him to the apostles." This act alone reveals that Barnabas views Paul as a promising, talented prospect, just waiting to be used of God in tremendous ways. Paul may have felt a little silly. After all, one minute he is zealously attacking Christians and the next he is trying to convince them that his heart is changed. I can hear Barnabas saying, "Paul, God has laid His hand upon you and called you for a special purpose. This is no accident or coincidence. Let's go to the apostles so you can share your testimony with them. They will see that you are now a follower of The Way and that God desires to use you in a mighty way." Wouldn't you like to have a Barnabas in your corner constantly uplifting and encouraging you, always seeing the potential you possess rather than counting up the failures in your life?

When the gospel spreads to Antioch with a report of many new converts, the apostles send Barnabas to verify the genuineness of the situation. Upon confirming the Spirit of God at work, Barnabas travels to Tarsus with the hope of finding Paul and bringing him to Antioch. Paul is a powerful teacher and understands the Greek mind and culture. Paul is perfect for the situation.

Barnabas, the optimistic encourager, takes an interest in Paul, encourages him, and prods him along toward fruitful ministry (Paul penned a good portion of the New Testament). Surely the encouragement of Barnabas plays an instrumental role in Paul's spiritual accomplishments.

Quite different from Barnabas is Timothy, who represents a protégé, someone to receive guidance and direction. Paul's writings showcase the guidance and direction he provides to young Timothy, whom he thinks of as his spiritual son. Paul is the wise and experienced mentor, while Timothy is the young and inexperienced mentoree. Paul draws Timothy under his wings and provides essential teaching, guidance, and direction. Paul invests in the life of Timothy, models successful ministry for him, and entrusts him with experiences that form and mold him.

I have seen plenty of "Timothys" in every congregation waiting for the "Pauls" of this world to gather them under their wings. With so many "Timothys" out there, it is physically impossible and unrealistic for pastors to handle this task alone; yet, it *is* possible and even desirous for every Christian to be involved in some form of mentoring. When we remember that mentoring is how Jesus taught His own disciples, it seems to be a worthwhile endeavor and a solid investment of time. You can probably think of one person right now whom you could consider a "Timothy" in your life. To always be the recipient of what others offer is a lopsided view of servanthood. The other side of the coin involves sharing with others what we have freely received. Investing our time and energy in another is certainly in keeping with the Christian ideal.

Take a moment to reflect upon your own life. Can you recall individuals who became a "Paul" to you, who invested themselves in your life? You are a better person because of their investment of time and energy, aren't you? Just thinking of them brings fond memories and precious moments to your mind.

Epaphraditus, the last member of our trio, represents someone to enjoy on a peer level. In Philippians 2:25, Paul calls Epaphraditus "my bother and fellow worker and fellow soldier." They are colleagues in ministry and possess deep compassion for those they serve. Paul recognizes how much Epaphraditus longs for the Philippians and notes that Epaphraditus "was longing for you all and was distressed because you had heard that he was sick" (Phil. 2:26). Paul and Epaphraditus are ministry peers with like-minded compassion. We find them sharing with each other as Epaphraditus brings Paul supplies sent from the Philippians (Phil. 4:18).

Some have equated Epaphrus, an imminent teacher in the Colossian church, with Epaphraditus, believing Epaphrus to be a shortened version of Epaphraditus. If this is true, we gather even more insight into Epaphraditus. If Epaphrus is a totally different individual, then we find another peer with whom Paul shared his life. Either way, they are like-minded colleagues sharing and caring for one another.

Having a fellow soldier whom you trust, hold in high esteem, and feel comfortable sharing with is worth its weight in gold. For those in full-time pastoral ministry, professional jealousies may arise that inhibit these types of relationships from forming. Ministers of small rural churches may feel that large metropolitan pastors don't care or understand their situation. Pastors of large, multiple staff churches may feel disconnected because they are viewed as having finally obtained ministry success.

Professional jealousies have infiltrated my own experience as a minister. Others were jealous of my level of education, my public speaking skills, and the publishing of books. Believe me, countless individuals exhibit much greater talent, skills, and gifts than I possess. My role is to be faithful to the abilities God has given me. Yet, it goes to show that unfounded jealousies, stereotypes, and prejudices can become barriers to enjoying one another's company.

Despite the potential barriers, it is possible for like-minded colleagues to interact on a peer level. Not every individual you consider a peer will be trustworthy and willing to jump over relational and professional hurdles to experience mutual edification. The key to this kind of successful relationship is not so much that one is a peer, but that one is a *trusted, like-minded* peer, willing to both give and receive in the relationship.

With colleagues in the same profession, a common understanding and knowledge base exists upon which to build a relationship. Both individuals have "been there, done that," and wasting precious time trying to figure out what the other person is experiencing doesn't occur. When a common knowledge and experience base is combined with healthy doses of mutual respect, trust, and honesty, the potential for a successful peer relationship takes on new dimensions.

Do you have a Barnabas in your life? Is there someone who provides a steady flow of encouragement and emboldens your potential? Do you have a Timothy in your life? Is there someone who could benefit from your wisdom, direction, and guidance? This is an opportunity for you to share with others what God has taught you. Finally, do you have an Epaphraditus in your life? Is there someone who understands your corner of the world with whom you can trust, share, and enjoy on a peer level? If we all had a Barnabas, Timothy, and Epaphraditus in our life, the entire Christian community would be transformed and elevated to new heights.

Influencing Others

Every individual on the face of the planet has been influenced by someone. The influence of others upon our life, to a certain degree, affects who we are as a person. Despite having our own temperament and personality, how we act, react, and perceive certain situations is impacted by significant others around us.

Pre-marital counseling, for instance, is a good case in point. During the first session, I review the purpose, need, and benefits of pre-marital counseling. I find that women are typically eager to learn all they can in order to better the relationship, while men often endure the session with glossy eyes. As they stare out the window and yawn, they convey nonverbally, "This is a big waste of time."

When I share these typical responses with couples, we all have a good laugh, which leads me right into the need for counseling. We discuss how the influence of others affects their own relationship. For instance, role expectations, conflict management styles, communication habits, and financial management are largely the result of others' influence upon us. If the finances were handled exclusively by the father in the bride's family and exclusively by the mother in the groom's family, expectations surrounding this area could become problematic if not properly addressed. Our actions and reactions are shaped and molded as we grow up observing the behavior of those closest to us.

Not all of the influences we receive are positive. If mom always acquiesced during marital arguments, it is possible that her daughter will react in a similar manner, or her son may expect his new bride to acquiesce in the same manner. An inebriated father who beats his wife in front of the children is undeniably providing a negative influence. Constant criticism and the downing of others is never productive and scars people deeply. Too many negative influences act as barriers to a healthy life and hinder our attempts to become all we can be for the glory of God. No person is a lone island, disconnected from others. Whether we admit it or not, our actions and behaviors are not isolated events—they actually do affect others, hopefully in a positive way. Honey catches more flies than vinegar. Similarly, positive influences have the capability of impacting people for life. Positive influences can turn a caterpillar into a butterfly and a frog into a prince.

I remember watching the final game of the 1993 National League baseball playoffs. Curt Shilling, Philadelphia's winning pitcher and MVP recipient, beat Atlanta in the final game of the series. As the MVP award was presented to him during postgame ceremonies, I couldn't help but notice how many times he praised and thanked his father for setting a noble example, showing him the importance of discipline and hard work, and encouraging him to set his sights high. In his moment of fame, this MVP pitcher publicly acknowledged the positive influence his father had upon him.

The life-changing effects of affirming influences is easily seen in Ann Mansfield Sullivan, who was hired by the parents of Helen Keller to teach their blind and deaf seven-year-old child. The story of Helen Keller and her contribution to society is well known, but a snippet from Miss Sullivan's journal reveals the power of influence: "My heart is singing for joy this morning. A miracle has happened! The light of understanding has shone upon my little pupil's mind, and behold, all things are changed." [10]

CHARACTERISTICS OF GOOD MENTORS

The purpose of this book is to encourage the investment of your time, knowledge, and experience into others so they can become their best. If your desire is to constructively influence people, you may be interested to know that there are characteristics common to those who successfully and positively mark the life of another.

1. Good mentors see potential in others.

All people, no matter who they are or what they have done, have potential within them. While some have more than others, everyone can improve in some phase of their existence. People who influence others have an ability to spot aptitude and bring it to the surface. It is far too easy to view others as barriers in our path instead of individuals with the capacity to become better. I fully recognize that within the church, there are those whose behavior, either knowingly or unknowingly, is a hindrance to the body of Christ. Their nature is consistently antagonistic, and one wonders whether they are true believers or not. Though they create whopping heartaches for the church, we find solace in the fact that their numbers are small. For the most part, people are merely big bundles of potential waiting to grow and expand. How we view others affects how much influence we have upon them.

While Jesus is in Bethsaida a blind man is brought to Him for healing. Mark 8:23–25 records the event:

> Taking the blind man by the hand, He brought him out of the village; and after spitting on his eyes and laying His hands on him, He asked him, "Do you see anything?" And he looked up and said, "I see men, for I see them like trees, walking around." Then again He laid His hands on his eyes; and he looked intently and was restored, and began to see everything clearly.

When others are viewed as "walking trees" that keep us from attaining our goals, we too are in need of a second touch from the Master. Troublesome individuals have the capacity for growth, spiritual expansion, and positive impact. Sometimes the problem is not so much "walking trees" as it is our skewed perspective. When viewed as bundles of budding possibility, others are freed from the bondage of our limited vision.

Jesus sees promise in individuals. Although scores follow Him, His exclusive attention is limited to training twelve individuals. He unleashes the potential within them, and their lives are completely transformed. He sees hope in Mary, Nicodemus, and the woman at the well. Jesus is the type of person who points out possibility. He believes that God's grace and power can lift us far above the mundane drudgery of mediocrity and move us toward significance.

With God all things are possible (Mt. 19:26). Think of yourself as a vessel of bundled potential. Once you were far away from God, but He changed you into a new creation. He recognized your promise and delivered you from the kingdom of darkness to the kingdom of His beloved Son (Col. 1:13). He knew what His power and grace could achieve in you. In a similar manner, He intervenes in Saul's life while on the Damascus road and converts him from a misguided persecutor of the church to the most prolific author in the New Testament.

Think of those individuals who have most positively influenced you. Did they constantly down you, criticize you, and scream that you wouldn't amount to a hill of beans? No, because that type of influence never brings out latent ability; it only straps you down. Influencers are those who see something in you, give you a chance, believe you have more in you than you ever dreamed, and help draw that potential out. They see a diamond in the rough while others view you as a lump of coal. These are the kind of people who supportively influence others and make excellent mentors.

Many do not have the ability or desire to acknowledge capacity in others. Sometimes this refusal is nothing more than insecurity and poor self-esteem—the only way they feel good about themselves is by bringing others down, or keeping them on a lower rung of the ladder. But if you really desire to mark a person's life through mentoring, remind yourself to always look for the promise in others and seek to draw forth their latent potential.

2. Good mentors exhibit enormous amounts of patience.

Another common characteristic of good mentors is their ability to display enormous amounts of patience and tolerance with others. This is one of my favorite characteristics, not because I am proficient in this area, but because I am not. In my own life, I pursue competence and sound reasoning. As my friend Bill Bygroves, Pastor of Bridge Chapel in Liverpool, states, "Perfection is my goal, but excellence will be tolerated." I demand a great deal from myself and often expect the same from others. It is wonderful to work hard, set high standards, and pursue excellence, but expecting the same from others can be problematic. Although I have made exceptional progress in my ability to display tolerance and patience, it appears to be an ongoing challenge.

Like many freshmen in full-time ministry, my people skills were a bit rough around the edges. Although I possessed an intense desire to serve God and others, I viewed certain individuals as hindrances to the movement and direction of God. My spiritual six shooters were at my side, loaded and ready to fire. Armed with the best of intentions, my pursuit of excellence was often construed as impatience and intolerance.

One of my mentors possessed amazing relational skills. People were relaxed around him, and he felt comfortable in their presence. They quickly sensed his wisdom, sincerity, and eagerness to listen. He modeled his relational craft right before my very eyes. I observed his skills and tried to improve my own abilities. Like clay on a potter's wheel, my mentor patiently worked with me. He tolerated my abrasive episodes without rejecting me until patience had its timely effect. He planted a seed, watered it, pulled treacherous weeds, and finally watched me blossom. His joy would have never been realized had forbearance not prevailed. He was willing to tolerate my unrefined behavior in order to see the promise within me come to fruition, and he knew that time and experience would work in my favor.

It was not until my next church that I realized the success of our mentoring relationship. My administrative assistant remarked, "You sure know how to read people. You're so kind and nice to them. I don't know how you put up with them. I would never have the patience!" Although she spoke these words to me, the compliment was really a tribute to my mentor and his ability to serve up generous portions of tolerance and patience in helping his mentoree develop.

Within the realm of everyday living, child rearing provides a superb example of the need for patience and tolerance. Those of you with little ones running around know exactly what I mean. If your children are now adults and on their own, you may recall instances where a little more patience and tolerance could have been exercised in your parenting endeavor.

Whenever I travel back to my home town in Iowa, it is my custom to always eat a Maid-Rite hamburger (alright, so I eat more than one). Maid-Rites are loose-meat hamburger steam-cooked with special seasoning and placed on an oversized bun (called Jumbo-Rites). Add a dab of soft cheese, and they become Cheese-Rites. To this blue-collar Iowa boy, they are mouth-watering delicious. Despite their pleasing flavor and addictive tendencies, they can also be exceedingly messy. That's why they give you a spoon with your sandwich, to scoop up all the loose meat that falls from the bun.

I wanted my children to try this fine Iowa cuisine that made dad's tummy dance with joy. My daughter did fine, but my son, all six years of him at the time, was having trouble holding the bun. Every time he attempted a bite, the loose hamburger spilled out in heavy doses. He wasn't holding his bun correctly, so the loose hamburger spilled out. I not only *told* him of the preferred hamburger hold, I *demonstrated* it for him several times. It was really a simple matter, yet he wasn't able to master "the hold." He began to cry and didn't want to finish his hamburger. My behavior toward him revealed intolerance and impatience with someone I loved deeply. Imagine how my heart ached when the next time we traveled to Iowa, my son did not order a Maid-Rite. The problem wasn't that he didn't like them; the problem was that he didn't want to put up with me riding his back for an incorrect hamburger hold.

The message reached me loud and clear. The next time we stopped for a Maid-Rite, we went ahead and ordered him one, chuckled at how daddy reacted the last time, and patiently worked with his "holding" ability. When the loose hamburger fell out of the bun, we laughed together. Now he eats

Maid-Rites all the time, and you know what? He eats them "right." A little tolerance and patience goes a long way.

In her early years, my daughter, Natalie, loved to assist with house-cleaning chores. Most often, she did more messing than she did cleaning. With tolerance and patience we allowed her to make mistakes, miss dust balls here and there, and feel as if she made significant contributions to household duties. When we taught her new techniques and suggested new responsibilities, she was receptive because our suggestions were offered with love and acceptance. If we model tolerance and patience with our children, there is a greater chance that they will model tolerance and patience with their own children in future years. When this trait is present in relationships, our influence upon mentorees becomes significant.

When you think of those who have most influenced your life, odds are that they exhibited generous portions of patience and tolerance. If you desire to be a mentor who influences others, don't forget to liberally apply patience and tolerance with mentorees.

3. Good mentors build up and encourage others.

The third common characteristic of good mentors is the ability to build up and encourage others. We are referring here to honest encouragement, not flattery or conniving conversation. Encouraging others to pursue a professional singing career knowing full-well they can't carry a tune in a bucket is to promote frustration, unrealistic expectations, and false hopes. Instead, encourage where you see *honest* potential. I am constantly amazed at what a little bit of encouragement can do for someone. Sadly, we often find ourselves swimming upstream in a surge of negativity. Let's be honest—one reason encouragement doesn't freely flow is that we sometimes don't want anyone else to get ahead, climb the ladder higher, or outshine us. After all, we reason, nobody encouraged us, so why should it be any different for anyone else.

Despite the positive message Christianity has to offer, churches are often viewed as cesspools of criticism instead of bastions of encouragement. I heard one well-known religious speaker remark that in his home town, one could find more honesty and encouragement at the local bar than at the local church.

This is quite surprising when one considers the "one another" texts in Scripture and the many passages exhorting us to build up and encourage each other. I cannot emphasize enough the importance of encouragement in the mentoring relationship.

A woman from a sister church in another town called to inquire if I would visit a family from their congregation who happened to be in our local hospital. The details of the horrible accident came to light as I began asking questions. Three teenagers were riding home from a beer party when they lost control of their pickup truck. The young teenage driver was dead at the scene, while the other boy escaped with minor injuries. It was the family of the third teenager that I was called to visit. Their seventeen-year-old daughter, Janie, was thrown from the sunroof of the truck and landed hard on the pavement. With bits of glass lodged in her partially exposed brain, she was flown by air ambulance to our local hospital.

Janie was in bad shape and wasn't expected to live. The talk of the hospital centered on how useful of a donor she would be. Even if she was to survive, there were lingering questions about the quality of her life. Would she sustain permanent brain damage? Would she be paralyzed? No one knew. While Janie desperately clinged to life in the intensive care unit, her mother pointed out and explained to me all the wounds she suffered.

To make a long story short, Janie regained consciousness and made a miraculous recovery. It did not come quickly or easily. There were painful skin grafts, relearning how to talk and walk, along with endless hours of physical therapy. It was difficult and frustrating work.

I share this story simply to say that I believe Janie's recovery would not have occurred as quickly or fully had it not been for the constant encouragement of her family and friends. Mom was constantly by her side reading Scripture, playing Christian music, sharing greetings from friends, and being a constant cheerleader during those long hours of rehabilitation. I saw firsthand the power of encouragement in Janie's life. I recall the heartfelt joy I experienced when she walked into church to worship with us one Sunday morning. Her journey from near-death to precious health was nursed along by encouragement.

Remember this important quality as you mentor others. Be an encourager instead of a fault-finder. Mentorees will respond confidently to your constant encouragement and someday experience the overwhelming joy I felt when Janie came walking into church on that blessed Sunday.

4. Good mentors see the big picture.

The fourth common characteristic of good mentors is perspective—that is, seeing the big picture. They see down the long road and take into account the entire issue instead of only one tiny segment. They utilize a wide-angle rather than a telephoto lens.

Mentors help mentorees maintain balance and perspective. Let's say, for instance, that Beverly (your mentoree) desires to move from point A to point B. It is a laudable goal and certainly one worth attempting. She is chomping at the bit to get moving. As someone with a wide-angle perspective who has been down that road before, you realize the kind of forethought necessary for a successful endeavor. You know firsthand the specific pitfalls along the path from A to B because you fell into some of them yourself. You also realize that if specific outside influences arise, the path from A to B may actually turn into a detour from A to C to D before arriving at point B. Taking into account the whole picture allows you to suggest further preparation, encourage a rethinking of strategic plans, offer alternative routes, and provide wisdom for the journey.

Good mentors perceive the entire pie, not just a slice of it. They step back and view situations from a panoramic viewpoint, rather than with tunnel vision. A mentor with perspective can make helpful suggestions, bring up points that would otherwise be circumvented or ignored, and help mentorees consider essential, but overlooked, information.

For the sake of receiving a one-hundred-fold return, one young man was determined to invest $100 in the ministry of a well-known religious figure whose ministry has since gone down the drain. By giving $100 dollars, as the slick television con artist suggested, God would bless him with $10,000 dollars. He sure could use $10,000 dollars and thought this was a wise and biblical investment.

This gullible individual, however, only saw a thin slice of the pie without critically thinking about the other pieces. His selective perception allowed him to only see what he wanted to see. When my opinion was asked for, I tried to help him see things from a larger perspective. Unfortunately, he merely wanted me to validate his unsound reasoning and donation of $100 to the crookster. I began framing the issue within a larger environment. Had he taken into account the purpose of giving? Had he carefully examined his motive for giving? Were his emotions aligned with his intellect? Should he gather a little more information about the ministry? In other words, I began providing perspective on impulse giving and asked that he take into account all of the facts, not just his desire to earn a quick return on his money.

As it turned out, he donated $100 to this charlatan, fully expecting to receive $10,000 dollars. Of course, he never did receive his anticipated bounty. It seems to me that if this minister truly believed that one could reap $10,000 for every $100 given away, *he* should be giving away $100 bills to his listening audience. His ministry would forever be flourishing as he raked in thousands upon thousands of dollars for the low cost of only hundreds. Instead, we find him always milking others for $100 and never giving a dime away. While we watch the right hand of his magic trick, we miss the subtlety of his left hand in our pocketbook.

Just because mentors provide perspective does not necessarily mean mentorees will accept it. This is where patience and tolerance comes into play. Allowing others to make mistakes is part of the maturation process. Mentorees, on the other hand, must be willing to listen and evaluate the experienced information of those who have traveled the road before them. When entering into relationships, remember to provide mentorees with big-picture perspectives that take into account the whole and not merely the parts. In doing so, you become an excellent example of reflective and evaluative thinking, and you may possibly produce in the mentoree a lifelong habit of seeing both the whole *and* its parts.

5. Good mentors are resource guides.

The final characteristic of good mentors is the ability to be a resource guide for mentorees. Information is powerful. The army with the most knowledge of troop movements, weapons used, and enemy plans has a decided advantage for winning the war. Realizing the power of insider information in the stock market produces a distinct financial advantage and is illegal in the United States. Police departments and federal agencies spend millions on cutting-edge technology to gather and analyze evidence. This highly technical information provides an advantage in catching and convicting criminals.

The power of information was acutely brought home to me when my wife was pregnant with our first child. While at the doctor's office, she asked a specific question that weighed heavy on her heart. To me, it seemed like a trivial question so I said, "Oh honey, don't worry about that." Astounded by my impudent remark, the doctor replied, "As a minister, you should know that people don't quit worrying because you tell them not to; they need information and facts to alleviate their fears." My wife was simply attempting to ease her apprehension by gathering proper information, and once obtained, her fears subsided. That little incident is forever etched in my mind, and it taught me a valuable lesson regarding the power of information.

Information comes in a variety of forms, such as timely advice. Mentorees often find themselves swimming in unfamiliar waters and facing situations they have never encountered before, or they are at a significant crossroad and decisions will impact their life for years to come. Critical junctures in one's life become opportunities for timely advice.

Lest we limit timely advice only to the eventful moments of life, we are reminded of its benefit in the routine of daily living. Family and spouse relationships, job pressures, time management, routine everyday thinking patterns, and our daily walk with the Lord are just a few activities for which timely advice is beneficial.

A story from personal life experience, an extraordinary quote, a fact, a book, or something else can serve as timely advice. Advice that comes at just the right time, precisely when it is sorely needed is timely. It hits the nail squarely on the head and scratches exactly where the itch is located. This kind of advice is highly effective and is remembered and treasured, for it arrives at just the right time. Good mentors find ways to get useful information into the hands of mentorees, such as personal experiences, pertinent letters, newspaper stories, magazine articles, books, or other forms of literary information.

The mentors in my life have been living reservoirs of information. I probe them for book titles, magazine articles, and the names of individuals with whom further exploration of a specific topic can occur. I unashamedly probe them about their own personal experience in order to glean useful information. In fact, a large portion of what I have learned in life has come from gathering information from others. I seek knowledge because I understand its value upon my life. To think that we have reached the pinnacle of understanding is sure proof that we have not—we are never too old to learn.

Mentors who influence mentorees act as a repository of appropriate and timely information. To act as a resource guide is quite different than actually doing the work for mentorees. You can point out an insightful book but you do not have to read it for mentorees—to do so would be unwise and lead to dependence instead of independence.

Unfortunately, I meet individuals with high levels of competence, and instead of sharing their knowledge, they hoard it and protect it with an iron-clad determination to be one up on everyone else. They have no desire to build into the lives of others and merely look to stroke their own ego and protect their turf from outsiders. Top-notch mentors are so internally secure that they have no ego to stroke. They share their knowledge and experience so that others may learn and grow.

Since information is powerful, mentors often hold the key that unlocks doors to breathtaking panoramic vistas never before explored by mentorees. Do not fall into the trap of withholding information. The more generously you share the greater chance you have to influence others. As a mentoree, treasure the knowledge and information gleaned from your mentor's storehouse of knowledge.

Being a mentor is more than a title or a position; it is a relationship designed to empower another toward further growth and development. Mentoring relationships can be life-changing. To maximize your influence as a mentor, remember the five common characteristics of good mentors:

1. Good mentors see potential in others.
2. Good mentors exhibit enormous amounts of patience.
3. Good mentors build up and encourage others.
4. Good mentors see the big picture.
5. Good mentors are resource guides.

By possessing these characteristics, mentors distinctively mark mentorees for significant contribution within the kingdom. If you lack one of these characteristics, don't worry, you can learn them. In fact, you may need to find a mentor who possesses what you lack. When these five characteristics flow from your life, you find unparalleled success in positively impacting the lives of others.

CHARACTERISTICS OF BAD MENTORS

Just as there are characteristics common to all good mentors, there are also toxic characteristics common to bad mentors that are worth noting. I am hopeful that mentorees will be able to identify them and learn to avoid them. Frustration quickly mounts when mentors do not perform their function well. When this occurs, valuable time is wasted and emotional let-downs become commonplace as hopeful expectations are dashed. Recognizing the characteristics of bad mentors may protect you from enduring negative, disappointing, and frustrating experiences.

1. Bad mentors are always too busy.

Avoid mentors who are unwilling or unable to make room for you. Mentoring is a relationship that involves time, and there are only so many hours in a day. Mentors may initially be excited about the opportunity but soon realize they have no margin to devote to the endeavor. Because of time constraints, they find themselves in over their head and their "yes" really means "no." This results in broken promises, inaccessibility, and a deterioration of trust. There is no intention to maliciously mislead; they are simply unable to follow through on their commitment because of their busy schedule. When too many irons are in the fire, someone inevitably gets burned for lack of care. When this happens, any enthusiasm mentorees initially possess is soon replaced with mounting frustration, since they cannot receive the positive benefits the relationship is supposed to provide.

A distinction must be made between a person who is busy and one who is *too* busy. My mentors have been extremely busy. In fact, one of them, an attorney, worked a full day and frequently returned to the office from 9:30 p.m. to midnight. Not everyone can accommodate that frenzied pace; yet, we had no trouble finding time for our mentoring relationship. His commitment to me made room for accessibility. Although he maintained a hectic schedule, he committed himself to investing in me, and I am the benefactor of his commitment. We got to the heart of issues quickly and efficiently because we both realized the precious value of time.

Being busy is not a mentoring death sentence, but being *too* busy will most certainly choke off the relationship. You know someone is *too* busy when phone calls are never returned, scheduled meetings are canceled, and there is little accessibility in your hour of need. When too many irons are in the fire, mentorees can become a back-burner priority.

In seeking appropriate individuals to serve on my doctoral dissertation committee, I considered a very competent and qualified individual who happened to be the president of a large Christian organization. Although he was willing, his hectic travel schedule raised serious caution flags in my mind because I was working with established deadlines and a progressive pace of learning. Though he showed initial excitement, I knew I could not count on him. He could be out of the country inspecting a foreign mission work in Irian Jaya at just the time I needed him. I am not suggesting that mentors be available every moment of the day, but by selecting another individual, I avoided a potentially frustrating situation with a man who was *too* busy to meet expectations.

If you are presently in a situation where mentors are too busy for you, discuss this with them (as long as they are not too busy to discuss this with you). If no positive resolution follows, then graciously back away from the relationship and find someone else.

2. Bad mentors use you instead of help you.

The second characteristic of bad mentors is that they want to use you instead of help you. These individuals are far too excited for the relationship to begin because they view it as an avenue toward furthering their own agenda. Mentorees become sounding boards, a source of fresh ideas, and convenient companions when the mentor desires company. Instead of having your best interest at heart, these mentors delight in giving you extra work that they don't want to do. They see you as cheap labor—a gullible assistant helping to fulfill their own ambitions under the guise of mentoring.

While in high school I began taking flying lessons in a Cherokee Warrior, a nice plane. Instead of beginning in the usual Cessna 152 two-seater high wing, I could fly a four-passenger low wing aircraft for the same price. My cross country flights took me to destinations where my instructor conducted business. My input was never considered in deciding where our cross country flights might take us. I was young and didn't think much of it at the time; after all, he was the instructor.

Yet, I always had the feeling of being used on such trips. We flew to airports where he had to drop off an engine part or discuss a deal with someone. Instead of training me in the cockpit, he was filling out forms and preparing for his upcoming meeting. Once we were on the ground, he engaged in his business affairs while I waited in the plane. When I asked questions while in the cockpit, I felt I was interrupting his work. He took advantage of my young age and inexperience to promote his own interests. Instead of helping me, he used me. Needless to say, I quit taking flying lessons from him.

People who use you instead of help you make terrible mentors because they bypass the central ingredient of the mentoring relationship, empowering others for growth and development. If you find yourself in this type of relationship, discuss the matter openly with your mentor. If nothing changes, graciously back out and find another who genuinely desires to invest in you rather than promoting personal agendas. Good mentors have your best interest at the forefront of the relationship.

3. Bad mentors constantly criticize.

Avoid mentors who constantly criticize you. They are destructive. Criticism is a caustic acid that slowly erodes the pillars of relational strength. It is a deadly poison.

These mentors find it easy to point out why and how you are doing something wrong. Their position as mentor, they believe, grants them the right to point out your mistakes—*all* of them. Under this torrent of heavy artillery, it is not unusual for mentorees to feel they can never measure up to the barrage of nit-picky expectations. The irony is that they criticize you for not handling a situation like they would, yet, if you handled everything like your mentor, there would be no need for the mentoring relationship to exist. It is unrealistic and quite ridiculous for critical mentors to expect you to be like them. After all, you are in the apprentice position, not the master craftsman.

When criticism is the thrust of relational energy, praise is rarely forthcoming, and mentorees begin worrying more about pleasing the mentor than learning and growing. I have heard that it takes ten to fifteen positive comments to offset each negative comment, but I imagine the true number is much higher. *Mentors who use criticism as a tool of inspiration produce just the opposite of what they intend to accomplish.* Criticism can be extremely damaging.

A family bicycling together always had a wonderful time until they came to the infamous steep hill. The father rode his bike to the top and yelled for the others to follow. His wife remained at the bottom with their frightened son. This upset dad. He thought to himself, "My boy isn't going to be a sissy. He'd better conquer his fear now and become a man." Raising his voice in anger, he criticized his son for lacking the courage to ride up the steep incline. The father was doing what he thought was right, yet, it was turning out so wrong.

One weekend in late September, the father attended a conference where he learned that his criticism was having the exact opposite effect upon his beloved son. While he had the best of intentions, he was unaware of the destructive force of his disparaging words. That very day, he made a vow to stop criticizing and begin encouraging his son. It wasn't long before his boy rode his bike to the top of the hill. Bravo!

To rationalize the destructive nature of criticism, a euphemism has been created called "constructive criticism." This type of criticism is said to be good for us, and a few handpicked verses for biblical support are typically quoted such as Proverbs 15:31, "He whose ear listens to the life-giving reproof will dwell among the wise," and Proverbs 27:17: "Iron sharpens iron, so one man sharpens another."

The phrase "constructive criticism" is an oxymoron, like the term "efficient government," or "electrifying golf game." Rarely are governments efficient, and I have yet to watch a golf game on television that nearly made my heart stop. Though "constructive criticism" is absent from the Bible, it is often used as a justified means of telling others what we don't like about them.

I once interviewed for a senior pastor position at a church I eventually accepted, and during the interview process I asked church leaders, "In what ways do you encourage your pastor?" A senior elder, with years of experience under his belt, piped up and with all seriousness replied, "Well, we like to tell him what he is doing wrong." The watchdogs of criticism were barking loudly at this church, and its history revealed they had been barking for many, many years. What was I thinking in accepting this position?

When criticism becomes nothing more than me telling you how you don't measure up to my personal preference, my exclusive perspective, or my personal agenda for you, then it is anything but constructive. I believe the Bible teaches that the way to accomplish the best in others is through generous portions of encouragement. Difficult conversations may need to occur, but without unconditional love and acceptance in an environment of trust, it becomes destructive rather than constructive.

If you are in a mentoring relationship with high levels of "constructive criticism" and feeling that you will never be able to please your mentor, then graciously back out of the relationship and search for a new mentor overflowing with encouragement. Criticism is the hallmark of bad mentors. That which criticism touches, it spoils, and you will spend more time trying to avoid condemnation than cultivating growth.

4. Bad mentors are not with the times.

Avoid mentors who are not with the times. It is possible to find willing individuals with the time and interest to serve as mentors but who are out of touch with current issues and lack an understanding of the contemporary scene. These individuals are frozen in time with a philosophy and methodology that is disconnected from the real world of today.

Please do not misunderstand the point I am trying to convey. I am not implying that someone is out of touch with the real issues of today just because of age. In reality, my point has nothing at all to do with one's age; it has everything to do with keeping abreast of the issues, problems, and methodologies in one's field of study, interest, or profession. I personally know of many older individuals who are current with the times. Combine together their years of experience with their contemporary understanding, and they make wonderful mentors.

Years ago, my denomination utilized what was known as a "key city" approach to church planting. One simply located a "key city" which lacked our denominational presence, and an instant church was established. Land was acquired, a building purchased, and a parsonage procured, all without a congregation. A dark cloud of debt hung over the small congregation that finally formed. Their impact was minimal, and they spent more time trying to pay the bills than minister to others. The denomination realized the error of its way and no longer utilizes this church planting strategy.

If you want to find a mentor who understands church planting, don't connect up with one who still believes this method is the most effective. If you do, you will forever be spinning your wheels and learning a lot about nothing.

This antiquated method of church planting is certainly a worthy autopsy candidate for discovering its strengths and weaknesses in relationship to the larger issue of church growth, but mentors who believe this is an effective methodology keep mentorees far behind cutting-edge theories, methods, and contemporary thinking. Mentorees can be locked into outdated and ineffective systems when they yearn for learning applicable to today's world.

A careful distinction must be brought to light. When speaking of outdated thinking and behind-the-times practices, I'm not referring to the age-old, timeless, biblical truths, for they never change. I am referring to outdated methodologies and theories that struggle to relate to the ever-changing world we live in. We don't want to be selling buggy whips in a jet engine age. In short, find mentors who know what they're talking about and can relate their knowledge to the contemporary world of mentorees.

5. Bad mentors need their ego stroked.

Mentors in need of ego stroking perceive themselves as being a notch above everyone else. If you climb too high on the ladder of success, you might outshine them. They enjoy having a mentoree, but they certainly wouldn't want you producing greater impact or endangering their spotlight. They are hoarders of self-adulation. When mentorees are quick learners who show boundless potential, these mentors limit, stifle, and manipulate in order to prevent advancement beyond themselves. You can only rise so high because ego-mentors simply will not allow you to rise higher. They are protectionists who do what is necessary to preserve their status and turf.

This, of course, speaks volumes to their character and self-esteem. They have not yet grasped the fundamental principle of grounding self-esteem in God and our new status as His children. If God forgives us, redeems us, calls us His children, and accepts us, then the estimation of others is inconsequential. The opinion that matters most is God's opinion, and He says we are loved and accepted. When this fundamental, biblical concept is fully grasped and integrated, ego stroking is unnecessary.

The best mentors are those who feel totally comfortable in their own skin and have nothing to prove and nothing to hide. Who they are and what they have accomplished is recognized as coming from the very hand of God. They have received freely and desire to give freely. If God uses them to influence others and those individuals go on to attain more education, earn more money, accomplish superior results, and climb higher mountains, they rejoice in God's good pleasure instead of being overshadowed by a cloud of depression. Actually, good mentors receive immense satisfaction in playing a small part in unlocking the potential of mentorees and helping them shine brightly.

Just as there are good mentors, there are also bad ones. Good mentors become positive influences in the lives of mentorees. In like manner, bad mentors make a similar impression—a negative impact. Common characteristics of bad mentors include the following:

1. *Bad mentors are always too busy.*
2. *Bad mentors use you instead of help you.*
3. *Bad mentors constantly criticize.*
4. *Bad mentors are not with the times.*
5. *Bad mentors need their ego stroked.*

TEN COMMANDMENTS OF MENTORING

John C. Crosby, of The Uncommon Individual Foundation, developed a list of ten commandments for mentors of which I have added a few comments.[11]

Commandment 1: Thou shalt not play God.

This commandment reminds mentors not to think too highly of themselves. Their role is to influence and empower others for development and growth, not make their decisions, predict their future, or judge them.

Commandment 2: Thou shalt not play Teacher.

While we hope that learning occurs through the mentoring relationship, this commandment stresses the attitude or disposition of the mentor. One does not arrogantly say, "Me teacher, you pupil. I will teach you all you need to know." Teaching and learning occurs, but not like this. Rather, instruction follows the path of modeling, being together in relationship, and sharing information, insight, and experiences in an atmosphere of mutual respect. Jettison the "I know everything" attitude.

Commandment 3: Thou shalt not play Mother or Father.

Mothering and fathering tendencies merely increase dependence rather than helping mentorees stand on their own. Mentorees must learn how to make sound decisions on their own without the influence of a smothering parent.

Commandment 4: Thou shalt not lie with your body.

The emphasis of this commandment is congruity between nonverbal and verbal behavior. Nonverbal behavior such as slouching, crossing arms, lack of eye contact, and other body movements communicate far more than words can express. If eyes are twitching, feet are pacing, hands are fidgeting, and someone says to you, "I am very relaxed," would you believe them? Absolutely not! Their nonverbal language is incongruent with their verbal language. When the nonverbal and verbal behaviors are congruous, communication becomes trusted and believable.

Commandment 5: Active listening is the holy time and thou shalt practice it at every session.

Successful relationships involve a whole lot more listening than talking. Active listening conveys interest in what the speaker is saying. This involves "uh-huhs," head nods, eye contact, and numerous other nonverbal indications that you are listening. I disliked speaking with a particular individual because I never felt he listened to me. As I was speaking, his eyes were scanning the crowd or looking at his watch. I knew beyond a shadow of a doubt that he found me to be a very uninteresting individual. I could have stopped in mid-sentence, and he would have never known. Active listening is a caring gesture that communicates warmth and concern. It is a nonverbal way of saying, "You are important and I will give you my undivided attention."

Commandment 6: Thou shalt not be judgmental.

This is the destructive criticism discussed earlier. The sweet nectar of encouragement attracts many more flies. Jesus addresses this judgmental attitude in Matthew 7:1–5:

> Do not judge so that you will not be judged. For in the way you judge, you will be judged; and by your standard of measure, it will be measured to you. Why do you look at the speck that is in your brother's eye, but do not notice the log that is in your own eye? Or how can you say to your brother, 'Let me take the speck out of your eye,' and behold, the log is in your own eye? You hypocrite, first take the log out of your own eye, and then you will see clearly to take the speck out of your brother's eye.

Commandment 7: Thou shalt not lose heart because of repeated disappointments.

This commandment identifies the patience and tolerance necessary for successful mentoring. We live in a broken world, and try as we might, we fall and stumble along the path. It happens to everyone, and we should not become discouraged. Patience and tolerance helps us rise up after each fall, shake the dust off our back side, and try again in the power of the Spirit. This commandment isn't referring to the dashed expectations and frustrations often experienced with mentors who are too busy or who continually criticize. The remedy for those kinds of mentors isn't patience and tolerance but graciously bowing out of the relationship and finding another mentor.

Commandment 8: Thou shalt practice empathy, not sympathy.

Sympathy is *feeling* sorry for others while empathy is *sharing* in their feelings and walking in their moccasins. People intuitively know the difference between someone merely feeling sorry for them and someone actually sharing in their hurts and joys. Empathy, not sympathy, enhances the role and effectiveness of the mentor.

Commandment 9: Thou shalt not believe that thou can move mountains.

Successful Christian mentors exhibit true humility and dependence upon God. Though they may be strong individuals, they humbly realize that anything they accomplish comes from the hand of the Lord. Only arrogance and misguided self-assurance causes mentors to think they can move mountains without the Lord's help. While God uses us in tremendous ways, all credit ultimately goes to Him. Mentoring is a three-way street involving God, mentor, and mentoree.

Commandment 10: Thou shalt not envy thy neighbor's protégé, nor thy neighbor's success.

We are not in competition with one another; we are spiritual brothers and sisters striving to live a life pleasing to our Lord. We measure life by our passion for the Creator and conformity to His will. When all is said and done, all other measures are insignificant and inaccurate. Bloom where you are planted and mentor those God sends your way.

7

MENTORS AND MENTOREES

SELECTING A MENTOR

Choosing an appropriate mentor can make or break the relationship. Care in the selection process helps reduce the chances of a disastrous mismatch. Here are some helpful guidelines:

1. Seek God's guidance and direction.

In situations where wisdom is sought, claiming the truth of James 1:5 is essential: "But if any of you lacks wisdom, let him ask of God, who gives to all generously and without reproach, and it will be given to him." Proverbs 3:5–6 bears another pillar of truth to lean upon: "Trust in the Lord with all your heart, and do not lean on your own understanding. In all your ways acknowledge Him, and He will make your paths straight." When searching for the right mentor, remember that God leads those who seek His wisdom and pursue His will. Call upon the Lord and allow His Spirit to direct you in the selection process.

2. Select mentors who share your philosophy of life.

Choosing mentors who share your basic philosophy of life also helps ensure a successful growth experience. This is not to say that diversity is problematic or that mentors must see everything our way. If that were the case why would we need mentors? Diversity is encouraged.

By "philosophy of life," I am speaking of the broad stroke pillars that hold everything else together. One's basic philosophy of life is the stable platform upon which everything else is built. Watching mentors model a skill, attitude, behavior, or attitude is an outflow of their basic philosophy of life. What is modeled may be of no interest or value to you if the foundation for such behavior is off the mark.

This is not to say that Christians can't learn from nonbelieving mentors. This frequently occurs in the secular work place quite successfully. If you are a bank teller learning how to appropriately count money back to the customer, the issue of whether one is a Christian or not is irrelevant. But when we talk about *spiritual* growth and development, there is little nonbelievers can teach us since their basic philosophy of life does not include God.

I wouldn't want a morally deficient popstar to be my spiritual mentor. If I want to learn how to gyrate on stage during a concert, the popstar might be helpful, but if I want to learn how to become more like Jesus, there wouldn't be much spiritual insight to be obtained since we are standing on two very different outlooks of life. Our value systems travel in opposite directions. One includes God; the other doesn't.

A good match between mentor and mentoree includes similar value systems. If a mentor values knowledge and education, but the mentoree feels both are a waste of time, it is more difficult to convey the importance of learning because a value rift creates a wall between them. The mentor and mentoree can have vast differences on nontraditional, public, or private education, the role of education in society, or even the quality and content of education in our nation. However, if they differ on a basic philosophy that the pursuit of knowledge is worthwhile, then a value chasm exists, creating a significant foundational obstacle to successful mentoring. By choosing a mentor who shares your basic philosophy of life, you will both be building from the same foundation.

3. Select mentors who possess what you are looking for.

Selecting a mentor who possesses what you are looking for assumes that you know what it is you need. This entails an objective evaluation of your life. Are you lacking knowledge in certain areas? Are you looking to develop new skills? Do you need to rid yourself of old habits and master new behaviors? Does your attitude require adjustment? Knowledge, skills, behaviors, and attitudes serve as four main categories for assessing needs.

Diving into self-examination when our lives are so complicated can be daunting. Breaking down our mentoring needs into several categories helps us to focus on one area at a time. These are not exhaustive classifications, and you can create your own additional sectors, but they do serve as a solid starting point for the searchlight of God's Spirit. While these broad categories can be broken down into smaller units of inquiry, the point is that they provide entryways for evaluating your mentoring needs.

Once your own requirements are inventoried, you can seek mentors familiar with your specific areas of need. If your prayer life is in shambles, find a mentor who intimately practices this much neglected discipline. If you require understanding of household finances, seek mentors who demonstrate expertise in this area. If you yearn to become more patient, seek someone who exhibits this desired quality.

Since the perfect mentor who knows everything is nonexistent, understanding your specific needs helps narrow the list of possible candidates. Once you determine the area of desired mentoring, choose someone who actually possesses the skills, knowledge, behaviors, and attitudes you require. You know what they say, "You can't give it unless you got it." In other words, mentors cannot impart what they do not possess. By knowing your own needs, your search for a mentor is narrowed to those who "have it and can give it."

4. Select mentors you genuinely respect.

It is much easier to learn from someone you look up to and genuinely respect. Taken to the extreme, respect places mentors upon a pedestal of idolized perfection. No matter how successful or accomplished mentors may be, I guarantee they are not perfect. Respected mentors, however, have reached a level of competency that makes them attractive to you. When they speak, you listen. When they instruct, you are all ears. You are ready and willing to soak in what they have to offer because you hold them in high esteem. Find mentors you genuinely respect, give them your full attention, and you will learn more than you could ever imagine.

5. Select mentors who will keep you on track.

Mentors provide insight, guidance, direction, and advice, and act as accountable partners in your growth. People tend to do what we inspect, not what we expect. It may not be enough for mentors to merely provide insightful comments; some sort of follow-up is necessary, even if it is simply a verbal reminder.

Depending on the mentoree's need and the nature of the relationship, some situations will require greater accountability than others, such as take-home assignments, readings, and close monitoring. Some relationships will be less intense with very relaxed accountability. The degree of accountability will differ depending on the purpose of the relationship, but make no mistake about it, people do what we inspect, not always what we expect. Knowing this simple principle helps you to choose a mentor who actually desires to monitor your progress and determine if you are on track toward fulfilling your goals. Proficient mentors keep you on track.

6. Select mentors who understand their role and have time to meet with you.

Admirable mentors understand their role and devote valuable time to the mentoring process. It is a frustrating experience to finally procure mentors who possesses the skills and knowledge you need only to discover that they are inaccessible. There just isn't enough time in their day to meet, for you are a tertiary concern—a back-burner priority. When mentors do make time for you, do your part. Be prepared, complete your homework, assimilate what has been taught, and ask questions that reveal you've thought deeply about the issues. Please your mentor with progress and commit yourself to the relationship. Make sure the mentoring relationship isn't neglected in your own life.

Just because individuals possess what you need and have time to meet with you doesn't mean they will make a good mentor. They must understand their own role in the relationship. This is a critical issue worthy of serious consideration when choosing a mentor. Explaining to potential mentors exactly what you hope to gain from the experience is a valuable idea. When everyone fully understands what is given and what is received, the roles of each party can be defined, the process determined, and the level of commitment agreed upon. Even though they may possess desired skills and knowledge, many mentors stumble in their influence simply because their role and function in the mentoring relationship was unclear from the beginning. Choose mentors who not only have time for you, but who fully grasp their role in the relationship.

7. Choose the best mentors possible.

Selecting the best mentor possible is the focus of this step. Don't allow fear or low self-esteem to thwart you from choosing less than the best available option. Often we say, "Oh, he would never consider mentoring someone like me." This predisposition often precludes us from attaining our end goal. If prospective mentors are unable or unwilling to accept the mentoring role, let that refusal come from their lips, not yours. When striving for the best mentor possible, don't settle too early for someone less than God's best for you.

While selling furniture to help pay for my seminary education, this prejudging phenomenon became crystal clear to me. I realized that many sales were missed because of a bias on the part of the salesperson. An elderly woman walked into the store one day and no one wanted to help her. They thought, "She's just an old woman. She'll never buy anything." I took time to assist her and wound up selling a day bed and mattress for her apartment. As it turned out, she actually lived in my apartment complex, and we became good friends. A predisposition on my part would have led to a lost sale, and more importantly, a lost friendship. Strive for the best mentors possible, and if they say no, then at least you tried. But if they say yes, then you've found yourself an excellent learning partner.

8. Select mentors who see your potential and have your best interest at heart.

Wouldn't it be nice to have someone in your corner constantly encouraging you, someone who sees your untapped potential and has your best interest at heart? Find someone who can help turn your dream into a reality. Unfortunately, many folks have no one in their life willing to stir up their latent potential.

Everyone has aptitude for something, but bringing that latent ability to fruition entails much time and effort. To do this, mentors must make an investment of time, energy, emotion, trust, finances, and so on. Mentoring another always involves a measure of risk, and there are never any guarantees. Much like the stock market, it is possible to invest a large amount only to see your investment go down the drain. Are you worthy of someone's investment? It is a probing question, isn't it? As you seek "investors," choose individuals who perceive your potential and can elevate your expectations.

When mentors see promise in you *and* at the same time have your best interest at heart, the probability for a highly motivated relationship exists. After all, we are talking about *your* life and *your* development, so choose mentors who will champion *your* cause.

Stay away from those who need their ego stroked and who desire to use you instead of help you. Seek individuals who find joy in helping others succeed and are not threatened by the achievements of their mentorees. It is helpful to ask yourself if they are committed to *your* personal development and *your* best interests. Do they really believe in you, or are they merely using you for their own ends?

9. Select mentors who are transparent and can teach you.

Like crackers and cheese, teaching and transparency pair well together. The whole idea behind mentoring is to share God-given resources so others are empowered to be more like Jesus. One vital aspect of "sharing" is teaching. John C. Crosby reminds us in his *Ten Commandments of Mentoring* that "Thou shalt not play Teacher." [12] Yet, teaching occurs in the mentoring relationship and, hopefully, someone is learning something. What Crosby is guarding against is the smug "I-know-everything attitude."

Many mentors can *do* things well, but great mentors *show* others how to do it. Sharing skills, behaviors, attitudes, and knowledge with mentorees is teaching. Though some do this better than others, choose mentors who share in ways that make it easy for you to learn.

Being transparent enhances effective teaching. Transparency removes mentors from the pedestal of perfection and places them firmly on the crowded road of humanity. Mentors are not superheroes; they are simply individuals struggling like the rest of us who are willing to share what they have learned. They are not perfect, nor would they claim to be. They are regular people who possess something we desire, so we enter into a mentoring relationship with the high hope of possessing it ourselves. As mentors share their failures and not just their successes, we realize they don't have to be superheroes after all.

When mentors disclose their hopes, dreams, failures, and successes with transparency, confidentiality is essential. This private information is guarded in your hands. In other words, opening up to others involves risk. Transparent teachers accept this risk for your benefit. Honoring a code of confidentiality builds trust and allows for impressive exchanges of transparency and mutual edification. Don't waste your time seeking perfect mentors—they don't exist. Instead, seek those who not only possess what you are looking for, but who actually know how to teach it to others with genuine transparency.

If you wait for a mentor who exhibits all of these characteristics, you may be waiting a very long time. All mentors have scars, blemishes, and faults of some kind or another and may not measure up to all of these ideals. This list is not intended to be a disqualification checklist but a tool for setting your sights high in selecting the best mentor available.

In summary, the guidelines for choosing mentors include the following:

1. *Seek God's guidance and direction.*
2. *Select mentors who share your philosophy of life.*
3. *Select mentors who possess what you are looking for.*
4. *Select mentors you genuinely respect.*
5. *Select mentors who will keep you on track.*
6. *Select mentors who understand their role and have time to meet with you.*

7. *Choose the best mentors possible.*

8. *Select mentors who see your potential and have your best interest at heart.*

9. *Select mentors who are transparent and can teach you.*

SELECTING A MENTOREE

While mentorees look for individuals willing to share their God-given resources, mentors are searching for those worthy of their investment of time and energy. If you possess a God-given resource and are willing to share it with another, you may find the following selection guidelines useful. Choosing the right mentoree can make a world of difference in the quality of relationship you experience.

1. Ask for God's guidance and direction.

Why not begin with prayer? According to James 1:5, the all-wise and all-knowing Creator imparts wisdom to those who ask for it: "But if any of you lacks wisdom, let him ask of God, who gives to all generously and without reproach, and it will be given to him." From Genesis to Revelation, we see God leading His people. With the help of God's Spirit, it is possible to walk in step with His leading: "If we live by the Spirit, let us also walk by the Spirit" (Gal. 5:25). No matter how good a potential mentoree looks on paper, always seek God's direction in the matter.

2. Choose mentorees who are seriously committed to the relationship.

As a mentor, your time is valuable. Don't waste it on those unwilling to put forth a serious effort toward personal growth and development. Some may desire association with you for reasons other than learning and growth. Seek to discover their motivation. Do they understand the purpose of the mentoring relationship? Will they commit to the duration and time frame established? Is this a low priority in their life or will they take it seriously?

You are not asking mentorees to become your personal servant or to be dedicated to nothing else in life but mentoring. You are, however, attempting to discern if they are willing to put forth an honest effort in commitment, just as you are. It takes two people (mentor/mentoree) for mentoring to be successful. If one is nonchalant about the relationship, mentoring becomes an exercise in futility while frustration mounts for both parties.

3. Choose mentorees who exhibit potential.
Invest in someone you sincerely believe in. Select someone you believe can succeed—someone with potential for development and growth if they really work at it. If you think success is highly improbable, you will merely go through the motions with less than good faith efforts. To avoid this negative bias, some feel all mentorees should be treated as though they have vast reservoirs of capacity for just about anything. But is this a reality? Is it fair to mentorees?

If a famous artist invited me to be her protégé, I would be an overdose of disappointment as she quickly realized my lack of artistic promise. My artistic gifts border on the nonexistent. I'm not bad with circles and squares, but anything more complex is bad news. There are those, however, who would make excellent protégés because they possess some ability to draw. They think like an artist. They speak the language. They quickly grasp color theory, perspective, and all of those other things that make art, art. They gravitate toward the artistic and possess enormous amounts of potential ready to break forth.

My wife once drew a quick sketch of me that I felt was rather impressive. I snatched her sketch pad and asked if I might draw her. By the time I was through, which by the way didn't take very long, she looked more like a contorted alien rather than a member of the human race. We had a good laugh over my ineptness and agreed not to hang the masterpiece above the fireplace mantle. This little story illustrates the point well; some possess artistic potential, but it isn't my strong point. I could probably learn a great deal about art, perspective, sketching, shading, and the like, but I will never be able to draw like those with genuine potential. My wife possesses artistic ability and graduated with a Master of Fine Arts degree in painting. The graduate school recognized her promise and helped unleash her artistic abilities into exquisite form.

Even Jesus provides an example of mentoring those with potential. His selection of the twelve disciples is not a random process. They are not the first twelve people He happens to come across. He is specific and particular in His choice. Of all the people He could have chosen, why did Jesus choose these twelve? Robert Coleman, in his book *The Master Plan of Evangelism*, offers an explanation:

> Jesus saw in these simple men the potential of leadership. They were indeed "unlearned and ignorant" from the world's standard (Acts 4:13), but they were teachable. Though often mistaken in their judgments and slow to comprehend spiritual things, they were honest men, willing to confess their need. Their mannerisms may have been awkward and their abilities limited, but with the exception of the traitor, their hearts were big. What is perhaps most significant about them is their sincere yearning for God and the realities of His life. [13]

According to Coleman, Jesus perceives leadership abilities in the twelve. He sees their big hearts, their teachable spirits, and their sincere desire to know and experience the realities of kingdom life. Jesus chooses mentorees with potential for spreading His message. It is difficult to imagine a stinky fisherman with leadership promise, but Jesus looks on the inside. In like fashion, choose mentorees who have potential to succeed. What individuals with budding promise often need more than anything else is someone to encourage them and draw forth their latent abilities.

4. Choose self-motivated mentorees who enjoy challenges.

"Self-motivation," now that's a thought-provoking term! I discovered a long time ago that people tend to do what they want to do. In other words, they always find ways to be involved in those things that motivate them. No matter how hectic my schedule, I always found time to play basketball on Monday evenings in the church league. Why? Because I am motivated to get on the court and play basketball, run up and down the gym, sweat profusely, and feel that I am exercising my body.

Self-motivated people are a joy to mentor. As self-starters, they actively engage in the mentoring process and take the initiative in acquiring and implementing new knowledge and skills. They are proactive and stretch themselves to new heights.

The opposite of self-motivation is someone inclined toward passivity. Couch potato protégés are liabilities who need constant prodding, and when they finally get moving, they complain the entire way. Time, energy, and insight are often wasted on passive, unmotivated individuals. They expect mentors to do all the work, and this is unacceptable. Passive mentorees drain you, while self-motivated individuals are energizing and delightful. Once the kindling wood is lit, the fire continues to burn bright.

Self-motivated mentorees enjoy challenges. Since mentoring is about self-improvement, a desire for increased capabilities is not unreasonable. The apostle Paul was a self-motivated individual relentlessly pursuing the next frontier. Philippians 3:13–14 illuminates his desire to move forward in his walk with Christ: "I do not regard myself as having laid hold of it yet; but one thing I do: forgetting what lies behind and reaching forward to what lies ahead, I press on toward the goal for the prize of the upward call of God in Christ Jesus."

A self-motivated spirit for climbing newfangled mountains and exploring new frontiers is not hyperactivity. Yet, the process of spiritual growth and maturity, especially within the mentoring relationship, should present faith-stretching opportunities that move mentorees to new and deeper levels of understanding. As one retired military officer once remarked, "There is no comfort in the growth zone, and no growth in the comfort zone." Basically, if you are not challenged, you probably won't grow.

In our culture, it is far easier to sleepily sit by the spiritual fireside in our rocking chairs while pretending to be growing in our faith. What good does a large engine under the hood do if you only cruise down the interstate at fifteen miles per hour? Some mentorees like to remain in the wilderness while others desire to live in the Promised Land. The latter is the better choice.

5. Choose mentorees who are teachable and eager to learn.

A good portion of my life has been spent in senior leadership positions within churches and higher education environments. In both settings, I have been passionate about learning and teaching, spending countless hours helping others grasp concepts, acquire knowledge, and learn new skills. It took me a long time to preach through Ephesians, a book with only six chapters. Parishioners came with pencils sharpened and left with pages of new insights. It is my contention that individuals respond to situations and events according to their level of understanding. If this is true, then education and a teachable spirit take on entirely new dimensions.

Baseball was the sport I enjoyed most as a youngster, so when my own son was able to enter into organized leagues, I signed him up. His initial understanding of the game was shallow, and his play wasn't much better. As his knowledge of the sport grew, so did his skills. We constructed a pitching mound together, and he practiced his mechanics and became a solid pitcher. We sought out others with superior knowledge in order to learn from them and even purchased professional instructional materials. My son would never have attained his high level of proficiency without increasing his knowledge base.

My daughter, on the other hand, loathes the more physical sports and took up the graceful art of ballet. I will tell you one thing: while ballet looks simple, it is extremely difficult to perfect. With newfound soreness in her body, Natalie soon realized she had muscles she never knew existed. As I watched the effort she put into the craft, I was proud of her teachable attitude that enabled her to master new skills.

In 2 Peter 1:5–9, the apostle Peter instructs us to add knowledge to our faith:

> Now for this very reason also, applying all diligence, in your faith supply moral excellence, and in your moral excellence, knowledge, and in your knowledge, self-control, and in your self-control, perseverance, and in your perseverance, godliness, and in your godliness, brotherly kindness, and in your brotherly kindness, love. For if these qualities are yours and are increasing, they render you neither useless nor unfruitful in the true knowledge of our Lord Jesus Christ. For he who lacks these qualities is blind or short-sighted, having forgotten his purification from his former sins.

By maintaining and pursuing a teachable attitude, we do not become "useless nor unfruitful" in the kingdom. To remain in a static spiritual state is unhealthy. God fully expects us to grow, mature, and increase our knowledge.

After all, His divine power has granted us everything pertaining to life and godliness (2 Pt. 1:3). Increasing one's knowledge is a biblical concept, and maintaining a teachable attitude creates a receptive environment for learning.

Accumulating knowledge for the sake of knowledge is worthless in and of itself. The newly acquired information should be useful; it must find practical expression in our lives. The pursuit of knowledge and wisdom is a path that helps us to better live for God. It is not an end in itself.

Helping individuals who are eager to learn is invigorating. Those who lack interest or motivation drain you at a steady pace until the relationship deteriorates. Find mentorees who are enthusiastic and demonstrate a teachable spirit. Although they may not know *how* to learn, at least they are *willing* to learn. Your own commitment to the relationship is boosted when mentorees display this attitude. As a mentor, be sure to conduct an assessment of your own life to determine exactly what it is you are able to teach. Remember, you cannot give away what you do not possess. Know what it is you have to offer, and then teach it with all your might.

6. Choose mentorees who respect you.

The empowering process gets off to a better start when mentorees respect their mentors. To be a respected mentor, you must be respectable. One day your mentorees may become celebrated leaders, writers, or thinkers, but for now, they are looking up to you as someone who can help them grow. With respect comes an eagerness to learn. Without it, mentorees will most likely think of the relationship as some kind of "endurance test."

No one is perfect, and mentorees may not possess every item on this list. We must always leave room for the Spirit of God to direct us to individuals who may not be the model mentoree. These criteria are merely helpful guidelines in choosing appropriate mentorees and is not intended to be a disqualification checklist.

The guidelines for choosing mentorees include the following:

1. *Ask for God's guidance and direction.*
2. *Choose mentorees who are seriously committed to the relationship.*

3. *Choose mentorees who exhibit potential.*
4. *Choose self-motivated mentorees who enjoy challenges.*
5. *Choose mentorees who are teachable and eager to learn.*
6. *Choose mentorees who respect you.*

THREE VITAL DYNAMICS

This is an excellent time to introduce three vital dynamics necessary for successful mentoring relationships. When these three dynamics are present, a rewarding relationship is likely to occur for both parties.

Attraction
Responsiveness
Accountability [14]

Attraction

Attraction is the beginning point of any relationship. Mentorees don't randomly pick mentors out of a hat; they choose someone to whom they are naturally drawn. When two individuals linked together are not a good match, the transference of change is more difficult.

Learning is greatly enhanced when the principle of attraction is present. This is not a physical attraction, but a mental one. Attraction says, "I want to be in this relationship. I can learn a great deal from this person. This will be good for me." We are attracted to certain mentors because of their stand on certain issues, their knowledge and skills, their values, their positive attitudes, their personal experiences, their accomplishments, their character, their spiritual maturity, and a host of other things. Attraction translates into motivated behavior and eager attitudes. Without attraction, mentoring has a slim chance of making significant impact.

Responsiveness

Responsiveness refers to the willingness of mentorees to learn from their mentors. It is attitude translated into action. Mentoring relationships are like two-way streets; traffic goes both ways since two individuals must work together. A correct attitude is like an open door, inviting new knowledge and skills to walk on in.

The importance of attitude is seen in the realm of athletics. No matter what the sport, if athletes are convinced they will not or cannot win, they probably won't. Attitude affects motivation and performance. On the other hand, athletes who mentally say, "I can win. No one can beat me!" have a greater chance of performing well. Attitude correlates to motivation and performance. Simply put, a positive mental attitude is beneficial in life.

When attraction is present, positive outlooks are more easily acquired and mentorees have a greater chance of being responsive. When mentorees exhibit a learning posture, mentors experience a small slice of heaven. Who wouldn't want to mentor someone who demonstrates openness to learning and growth?

Accountability

Accountability keeps the relationship pure and on track by ensuring that learning and growth occur. A truism in life is that people tend to do what we inspect, not what we expect. The sharing of expectations, reviewing mentorees' work, monitoring progress, asking questions, and providing experiences help mentorees apply new learning to real life situations. Accountability is a way of saying, "This is where we want to go, this is where we are now, and this is what we need to accomplish if we are going to get there." A sense of meaning and purpose to the process exists when accountability is present.

Attraction, responsiveness, and accountability are all synergistically linked. It is sometimes difficult to discern where one ends and the other begins. Without initial attraction, there will be little responsiveness and even less accountability. This results in high levels of frustration and low levels of satisfaction. On the other hand, high levels of attraction lead to greater responsiveness and accountability. This, in turn, results in low levels of frustration and high levels of satisfaction. Attraction is an essential ingredient for successful mentoring. Without it, the mentoring relationship lacks sustaining power.

THREE VITAL DYNAMICS OF MENTORING

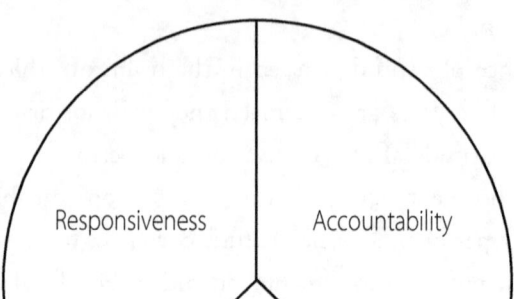

Mentors Need Mentoring Too!

Just because you become a mentor to another individual doesn't mean that you stop being mentored yourself. Reaching a state of perfection isn't going to happen in this life. For now, try as we might, we still exhibit flaws, need minor adjustments, and have plenty of work to do on ourselves. In other words, mentors will want to model the same learning posture they expect of their mentorees. It is both reasonable and beneficial to be mentoring another individual while at the same time being mentored ourselves. You can both mentor *and* be a mentoree at the same time. The cycle of learning never stops.

Since finding someone so talented and available to tutor all aspects of life is a rarity, the more practical scenario is to choose individuals with the skills and availability to mentor very specific areas. Over the course of a lifetime, it is possible to have many mentors because we never stop learning and our interests change over time. At age thirty, for instance, you may sense a need in the area of leadership. At forty, you may seek assistance with financial planning. At fifty, there is another need and another at sixty. Our goals change according to age, experience, and present circumstances.

The depth of our relationship with the Lord vacillates over time. The needs of new believers are quite different from the needs of mature followers. God uses life in its totality to shape and mold us, not just a specific time period. What I know now in my relationship with God is beyond what I knew ten years ago. My thinking and behavior have been revolutionized in proportion to my spiritual growth. I could not have progressed from point A to point Z had I not gone through the previous levels.

As we mature in the Lord, our relational depth with Him deepens. This means that our spiritual requirements also change. Different mentors help to meet these various needs. Over the course of a lifetime, it is probable and advantageous to be involved in many mentoring relationships, possibly several of them at one time. It is also not uncommon to both mentor and be mentored simultaneously.

My point is this: there are all kinds of mentoring relationships that may occur throughout a lifetime of progressive aging, changing ministry and work environments, shifting life situations, and evolving spiritual maturity. Because of the constant fluctuations in our needs, the kind of mentors we choose will vary as much as the needs themselves.

The type of relationship one has with a mentor is proportional to the need. Some relationships are more intense and require greater accountability because the need calls for it. While one relationship calls for highly accountable weekly meetings, another calls for monthly online meetings due to proximity issues. As with all relationships, there are varying levels of involvement and intensity depending on the circumstances.

8

LEVELS OF MENTORING

*T*here must be a better way to understand the various levels of involvement within the assorted types of mentoring relationships, all with differing lengths, subject matter, intensity, and so forth. There is![15]

The three levels of mentoring presented here may not be exhaustive, but they do help clarify the differing degrees of intensity. We often benefit by creating categories, divisions, or labels for clarification purposes. These labels act as handles of understanding allowing our mind to sort and digest information, and then store it away for future access.

It may be helpful to think of mentoring in three categories: intensive mentoring, occasional mentoring, and passive mentoring. As the terms suggest, intensive mentoring entails more deliberate involvement than do the other levels. Passive mentoring requires the least amount of commitment, while occasional mentoring is somewhere between the two.

The three vital dynamics of mentoring (attraction, responsiveness, accountability) are significant in the intensive level and less pronounced in the passive level, as the graph below suggests. The greater the intensity level, the greater need for attraction, responsiveness, and accountability.

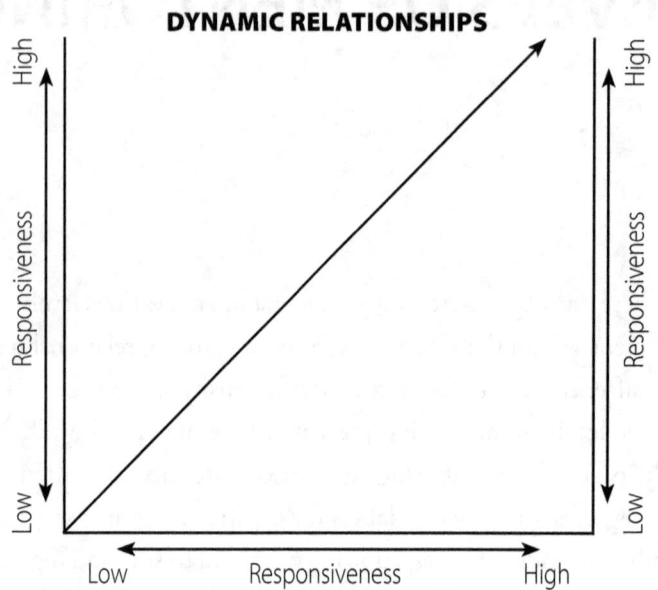

INTENSIVE LEVEL

The intensive level requires resolute dedication and commitment to goal attainment because its aim is serious change. Vast amounts of attraction, responsiveness, and accountability are necessary to sustain this relationship. Although fervid in nature, this level provides significant opportunities for attaining better results than the other two categories. "No pain, no gain" applies here. Sizeable achievements involve increased risk and hard work.

With its high degree of accountability, this level is not for everyone. Some just aren't ready for this kind of dedication. This is where the occasional and passive options come in handy with their reduced level of commitment. The three categories of mentoring means that everyone can be involved to some degree and choose a level that fits their lifestyle and passion. Is an intensive situation desired with its potential for yielding impressive results? Does a slower, more moderate approach to the subject better fit with identified needs and desired outcomes?

Stanley and Clinton, in their book *Connecting*, have further identified the various roles a mentor might perform in each level of mentoring. The intensive level, with its insistence on serious growth through strong commitment and accountability consists of three roles: discipler, spiritual guide, and coach. While these roles may not be exhaustive, they do provide insight into the function of mentors within the various mentoring categories.

Discipler

The term "discipleship" is very familiar to Christians, and a plethora of books abound on the subject. Often this word brings to mind a new believer's Sunday School class in which the basics of Christian living are addressed. Topics such as financial stewardship, prayer, Bible study, and witnessing are choice items on the menu. The Sunday School group meets once a week for fifty minutes with little or no accountability, although sometimes a one-on-one discipleship session occurs. New believers take home a booklet, look up Bible verses, and fill in the blanks of next week's lesson. Together, the group reviews the lesson answers, asks how things are going, prays, and returns home until the next scheduled meeting.

Accurately filling in the blanks and moving from booklet one to booklet five is viewed as discipleship. While this may be one aspect of discipleship, it certainly doesn't encompass the essence of the term. To me, simply filling in the blanks and memorizing facts is shallow and uninspiring in light of what discipleship really entails. The role of a discipler expands the boundaries of what most people commonly think of as discipleship.

Intensive mentoring involves a relationally based process—a more experienced and mature Christian building into the life of a mentoree. Keep in mind that Jesus teaches His disciples in a highly relational context that creates an environment conducive for learning. In like manner, the high level of commitment and accountability necessary in this level is best achieved in a relational environment. This is more than sending mentorees home to complete a lesson; there is an accountability factor whereby mentorees not only learn the basics of following Jesus but also gain valuable insight into such things as commitment, attitude, skills, and knowledge essential for building strong foundations of faith. Mentorees not only learn facts and observe their mentors' living examples, but they are held accountable to expressing the Christian faith in their own lives.

For instance, not only would mentorees examine the biblical teaching on prayer and observe their mentor pray, but they would also be expected to implement prayer in their own lives. They not only learn *about* prayer, but they actually pray. They not only learn *about* giving to the Lord, but they actually give, under the accountability and influence of their mentor. Mentorees not only learn *about* sin, but they recognize it and confess it. Our idea of being a "discipler" is not what many today call discipleship. Being a disciple involves a deliberate and intensive relational process that includes accountability. In this relational environment, mentorees learn the knowledge, commitment, and skills necessary for experiencing and following God. Mentorees not only expand cognitive abilities—they also implement real-life learning as they observe it, practice it, and are held accountable for it.

The majority of church-goers, in my opinion, have never been properly discipled. They may have attended a Sunday School class or finished a few booklets, but most have never come close to experiencing a relational process requiring commitment and accountability. I have no scientific, hard-core data to back my assertion, but when I ask people how they were discipled, I rarely receive a relational and accountable answer. Within the church, whenever I offer courses on the basics of the Christian faith, scores of believers who had been Christians for years clamor to sign up. Why? Because they don't have a handle on the basics. They have never really been discipled in a relational format and now find themselves floating on high seas without an engine and a rudder.

Longing for Biblical Discipleship

There are at least four important reasons why so many in our churches yearn for true biblical discipleship. The first reason entails the vast number of dysfunctional families in our society. For instance, there are more single-parent households now than at any other time in history. Broken families equal fractured relationships and because of this, families no longer function in the normal capacity God intended. Ministers witness firsthand the various issues that induce broken relationships, such as divorce, crime, gambling, alcohol and drug addiction, laziness, mental illness, infidelity, and so on. We often attribute such destructive behavior to those outside the faith and are slow to recognize its frightening presence within our own church walls.

In a humorous way, a cartoon in *Leadership Journal* captured the enormity of this problem. [16] The pastor is showing a new couple around the church, pointing out the various ministries as he walks. As they peek in on one of the groups meeting at the church, it is painfully obvious that there are only a small number of people present. The minister declares to the new couple, "And this is our newest support group, but by far the smallest." A sign on the door lists the name of the ministry group as "Adult Children of Perfectly Normal Parents." With the increasing number of dysfunctional families in our society, many long for stable relationships of trust—not merely a relationship that helps their faith grow, but a relationship that is also a positive experience for them.

Our experience with a relationally deficient culture is the second reason we crave biblical discipleship. Families don't have to be dysfunctional to be nonrelational. We live in a world where people don't know their neighbors and remain hidden within the walls of fortress homes. Metropolitan areas are much more prone to this than rural communities.

Many experience relational hollowness and have had enough of this "theology of distance." There is a new push in their lives to discover and experience meaningful relationships. Many are doing a turnaround, pursuing what they instinctively know is right and good for them, instead of succumbing to the mundane routines of contemporary society. Biblical discipleship provides a safe opportunity for experiencing both relationship and growth at the same time.

That many are turning away from the church's programmatic priority to a new emphasis on relationship within the faith community is a third reason we crave biblical discipleship. Sadly, whenever we seek to accomplish growth within the church, we search for, and establish, a program. Local congregations seek to purchase and implement just the right growth program. If they desire evangelism, a new evangelism program is introduced. If they want discipleship, they introduce a new discipleship program. This over-dependence upon programs leaves us dry and unfulfilled. It is entirely possible to have highly functional programs within local congregations and still be distanced from one another. People are beginning to realize that relationship, in and of itself, is worthwhile, and that growth in numbers without relationship is no success at all.

Programs are not improper or immoral and can be useful tools in kingdom work. As mere tools, however, they can never be anything but tools. The emphasis on evangelism, for instance, should be on relationships, not programs. Programs that lead toward relationships may be helpful, but unfortunately, the focus is typically on numbers. I wonder if our thirst for program evangelism has anything to do with our lack of dynamic fellowship with the Lord. Without a vibrant relationship with God, lifestyle evangelism becomes worthless, for there is nothing about our life that would attract others to our way of living. It is relationally difficult to share with others what we do not possess. It is much easier to master a program. In the early church, nonbelievers were attracted to Christianity because of the vibrant, living faith of Christians. A relationship with God for New Testament believers was life changing and clearly noticed by others. As a result, the church grew.

We are beginning to realize the deficiencies of programmatic approaches to ministry and are looking for relational models of evangelism, discipleship, ministry, etc. Instinctively, we sense something very special about the love and togetherness of first-century Christians. Average church-goers today are not concerned with winning a theological debate regarding issues in the book of Acts; instead, they yearn for the relational quality their predecessors in the book of Acts experienced. Modern-day believers sorely lack and sincerely yearn to experience relationship and community .

The deficiency of content in our learning becomes the fourth reason we crave biblical discipleship. Why do so many believers complete the fill-in-the-blank booklet series and still feel like they've gone nowhere? Though they master a few facts, they often experience problems with application and integration into the real world.

Could it be that not only the methodology, but the very content of those fill-in-the-blank books, are deficient? Bible study, prayer, giving, and witnessing are all important aspects of the Christian life, yet, there is other critical material for successful Christian living that may be missing. For instance, possessing a firm understanding of our new status as God's beloved children is a high priority. Understanding this new identity, especially as seen in the book of Ephesians, is a powerful instrument of attitude. Living life *based* on our new identity instead of trying to *achieve* a new identity is foundational content that is often overlooked! Why not also teach about the powerful influence of relationship upon our Christian journey?

People desire understanding and skills that help them live for God to their highest potential. This is best achieved through a relational process, not a fill-in-the-blank booklet. Mastering those skills takes time—much more time than a once-a-week Sunday School class provides. The discipler in the intensive level creates a deliberate, accountable structure for enhanced learning. This relational process allows for the modeling and practice of attitudes, perspectives, commitments, and behaviors. While the effort and time is weightier, the results last longer and produce better fruit.

Dysfunctional families, a relationally deficient culture, an overemphasis on programs, and deficient content in the traditional discipleship format are causing individuals to seek more relationally based learning experiences. While intensive disciplers cannot teach everything, they provide solid foundational structures that prepare new believers for the marathon of life.

Older adults in need of biblical discipleship may be reticent to acknowledge that their understanding and skill level are on par with new believers, even after so many years in the faith. How can we coax older Christians into a discipling relationship without offending them? One way is to utilize the three vital dynamics for successful mentoring relationships. Finding someone they are attracted to creates greater responsiveness, and with responsiveness comes accountability, no matter what the age.

Spiritual Guide

Mentors might also perform the role of spiritual guide in the intensive level. As the term suggests, these folks provide spiritual guidance for mentorees. The term "spiritual guide" has nothing whatsoever to do with what New Age teaching calls a spirit guide. In New Age philosophy, spirit guides are actual spirits who bring guidance to the seeker. There is no need for Christians to seek guidance from other spirits when the Spirit of God is readily accessible. When Jesus ascended into heaven, He sent the Holy Spirit to indwell, empower, guide, comfort, and lead us in paths of righteousness. While the Holy Spirit leads and guides in numerous ways, Scripture also encourages us to seek out individuals able to impart wisdom and advice. The Holy Spirit often places in our path those with greater maturity.

While in full-time pastoral ministry, my wife and I often initiated our own personal spiritual checkups, usually once a month. It was our spiritual buddy system. During this time we stepped back from ministry, and over an evening meal or late-night talk, we evaluated our spiritual walk and checked up on one another. Ministry has its ups and downs, joys and sorrows, glorious heights and grievous pitfalls. Always giving of ourselves, it was easy to become wounded in life's battles. Unless these wounds were promptly and properly cared for, serious infection could occur.

We checked up on our prayer life, personal time with the Lord, togetherness as a family, pastoral goals, ministry hot spots, motivation, attitudes, effectiveness, etc. We fully realized that to neglect our personal spiritual health would result in dulled ministry efforts and adverse effects upon ourselves and God's kingdom. These checkups kept us on the right track. To avoid bitterness and sarcasm, we forgave those who hurt us, realigned our attitude, renewed our vigor and dedication for service, and sought the Lord's healing, protection, and future blessing.

Our spiritual lives can be likened to a ninety degree angle. When we are out of alignment with God, we are improperly angled. The longer we go without correcting our path, the farther the distance between where we are and where we are supposed to be. The farther out from the vertex we go, the greater the correction needed to get us back on the right path. The best time to correct angle deviations is early on during the initial error. Caught early, the distance needed for correction is relatively mild, and left too long, the needed correction is enormous.

ANGLE OF DEVIATION

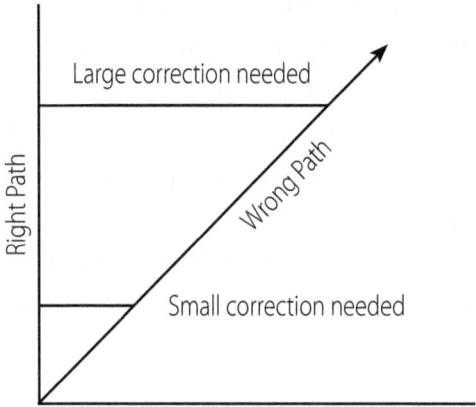

Through regular spiritual checkups, we can catch deviations early, quickly correct the angle of deviation, and realign ourselves with the Lord. Spiritual guides act as doctors who put their stethoscopes up to our chest and ask us to breathe deeply. As wise individuals with deep-rooted maturity, they desire to help us become more like Jesus by providing insight, answering questions, offering accountability, checking our integrity, and dealing squarely with motivation and attitude. Their focus is not to ground us in the elementary truths of Scripture as the discipler, but to spur us on to abundant spiritual growth and maturity.

During my college days, I went through a period of deep spiritual doubt and serious uncertainty. In many ways, I needed to question what I believed in order to own it for myself. My spiritual life had plateaued, and a philosophy course had me asking all kinds of ridiculous questions. Late one night, I met with a spiritual guide to discuss the situation and said, "I don't feel God's presence anymore. I feel like my prayers are just bouncing off the walls and going nowhere. Where is God? Maybe He really *isn't* there."

My friend knew I loved God deeply and possessed an intense desire to serve Him, and yet, he wisely understood that I was going through a phase. He did not chastise me, call me names, or shame me. Instead of lecturing me, he encouraged me. He cut to the heart of the matter and said, "Have you told God how you feel?" Those words hit me like a brick, and I realized that I was trying to commune with my Creator without being real before Him. Right then and there, we prayed together, and I told God exactly what I was thinking and how I was feeling about Him. It was a load off my chest. This questioning phase and spiritual plateau in my life actually deepened my trust and devotion to God. What would have happened if the spiritual guidance of a friend had not been there to lead me into deeper waters of faith?

Late one night, a dear friend called me for a spiritual checkup. He had been involved with his church for years, putting up with all kinds of disrespectful behavior from the congregation. Through thick and thin, he became the centerpiece God used to hold things together. He was weary of dealing with cantankerous people who seemed more interested in personal agendas than working together to impact their city. He desired purposeful ministry, but the congregation fancied gamesmanship. On the other hand, he realized that if he resigned, the congregation would be devastated. He finally came to the point where he was sick of it all. What was he to do? Stay, or leave?

For three hours, I played the role of spiritual guide for this pastor, examining Scripture, feelings, attitudes, thought processes, perspectives, needs, priorities, motivations, the church situation and a host of other items. My job wasn't to make decisions for him, but after his three-hour spiritual checkup, I felt assured that any decisions he made would be appropriate ones. The circumstances could have easily brought spiritual decline, yet through the spiritual guidance of a trusted friend during a critical juncture in his life, he turned the situation into a God-glorifying event. By holding him accountable, he grew in the Lord that day.

I am close to several treasured individuals, and we often play spiritual guide for one another. Our deep and sincere friendship allows us to risk being real with one another. This is a priceless gift between valued friends that doesn't occur with just anybody. By assessing the mentoree's spiritual life, spiritual guides help to deepen and expand their faith commitment. The wise discernment of these advisors become pathways for increased maturity. This may sound a bit like the discipler role, and while there are areas of overlap and both deal with the spiritual life, there are distinct differences between the roles. Disciplers deal mostly with bedrock issues of the Christian life and attempt to establish solid foundations upon which a successful Christian life can be built. Spiritual guides, on the other hand, typically deal with individuals who are beyond this basic stage.

Disciplers work with new believers since this is a pivotal time for laying solid groundwork while spiritual guides predominantly serve individuals who have clocked time in the faith. Disciplers seek to move mentorees from dependence to independence. Though they are a strong shoulder to lean upon for a season, mentorees must learn to stand on their own two feet. Spiritual guides move individuals from independence to interdependence. Not only must mentorees stand on their own when it comes to the basics, but they must also learn to positively interact with others once those basics are mastered.

It is not uncommon for disciplers to meet with mentorees for a fixed period of time. It may be six months or even a year, but when it is over, it is over. Disciplers then find other foundations to build—another new believer to invest in. Spiritual guides, on the other hand, can meet on multiple occasions with great periods of silence in between. When crucial life moments create rendezvous opportunities, meetings will be as often as these moments dictate. The number and length of get-togethers depend on the issues involved. Spiritual guides are there when you need them. Disciplers meet for the purpose of training, while spiritual guides meet for reflection and assessment of attitudes, motivations, behaviors, and thought processes.

Spiritual plateaus can become opportune times for spiritual guidance. When your passion is bone dry and you aren't moving forward, spiritual guides can be immensely helpful for an acute case of the spiritual blahs. Facing difficult obstacles is another occasion where the spiritual advice of another could be valuable. If your attitude is souring or you are becoming judgmental, it may be time for a spiritual checkup.

A low motivational gas tank may be yet another opportunity for seeking guidance. Spiritual guides often provide a balanced perspective tempered by years of experience. Another excellent opportunity for spiritual guidance is when you are in a place of influence and decision making. To lead effectively, a pure and right relationship with the Lord is indispensable. For the sake of others and yourself, seek spiritual checkups from wise and mature individuals.

Since life is more like a roller coaster ride than the sailing of smooth waters, we all need spiritual checkups periodically. My spiritual guides help in my moment of need and spur me on to persevere and positively impact others.

Coach

The last role mentors might perform in the intensive level is that of "coach." As the term suggests, coaches inspire mentorees to perform specific tasks. These relationships frequently occur when mentorees engage in new challenges, assume responsibilities in an area never before explored or mastered, or when a burden becomes too great to carry. Coaches who have been in the water before you are extremely beneficial when you're swimming in unfamiliar rivers.

Like a coach in any athletic sport, this relationship seeks to inspire confidence in athletes for improved performance. Coaches provide encouragement, feedback, and resources while striving to instill an "I can do it" attitude. They motivate players, aid in acquiring necessary skills for success, and assist in the application of those skills to particular situations. Whether bobsledding or basketball, coaches like to win, and they win by teaching skills and motivating players to higher performance levels. While athletic coaches often work with a team or group of players, mentoring coaches typically work with a limited few, usually in one-on-one coaching sessions.

The focus of a coaching relationship is to inspire, motivate, and teach mentorees to successfully complete or perform a task. To accomplish this, coaches utilize a process of observation, feedback, and evaluation. Skilled mentors are able to quickly determine where adjustments should be made while observing mentorees perform. These observations are shared with mentorees during feedback sessions and evaluation comes after the mentoree attempts to implement the feedback.

FEEDBACK LOOP

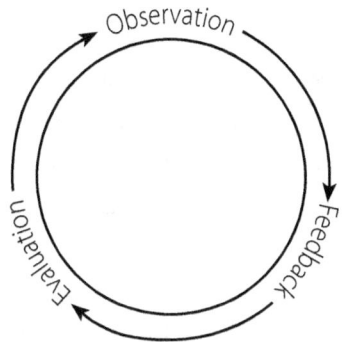

During my son's transition from Little League to Babe Ruth baseball, we searched for an experienced coach to help refine his pitching mechanics. While traveling to conduct a seminar, the woman sitting in the airline seat next to me boasted of a son who was the pitching coach for a college in Texas. To make a long story short, I ended up sending him pitching video of my son from all angles. We looked forward to receiving feedback from the coach since he had pitched college ball himself and possessed the critical knowledge we needed. His expert eye, we knew, would catch issues in my son's pitching motion that we were untrained to see.

If I were a golf enthusiast, it would be helpful to take lessons from someone who actually knew how to golf. My golf philosophy is as follows: if it goes left, it's a hook; if it goes right, it's a slice; if it goes straight, it's a miracle! That pretty much sums up my golfing knowledge. But if an experienced golfer observed me tee off, chip, and putt, I might actually be able to improve. He could observe my bad habits and gather information regarding my strengths and weaknesses. He would then share his observations with me through feedback. As I attempted to implement his feedback into my swing, he would further teach and correct me. After additional lessons and additional rounds of golf, I would like the expert to evaluate me again to see if I have successfully implemented new learning.

At times, I might think to myself, "I can't do this," but his encouragement and motivation would inspire me. The coach would not only teach me about correct golf swing mechanics, but he would actually model a correct swing for me. He may even provide further resources such as a good illustrative golf book or a tip on reading greens. This is exactly the kind of thing coaches do. Finally, on that day when my drive no longer slices and my lessons are over, the coach would have helped me play a much better round of golf.

This type of relationship is generally initiated by mentorees who recognize a need and seek out an experienced individual to coach them. It ends when the necessary skills are acquired. Remember, mentorees seek out coaches they are attracted to. There can be heavy doses of accountability within this relationship because both mentors and mentorees fully understand that to accomplish a specific task or successfully complete an important challenge, practice and discipline are required. Serious mentorees know there is a price to be paid for success.

While watching the Olympics on television as a young man, I decided to become a boxer. The medal rounds seemed to always involve the Americans and the Cubans. Sugar Ray Leonard was spectacular. The Spinks brothers captivated my imagination. Right then and there, I determined to be a boxer and win a gold medal. I envisioned myself standing on the winner's platform as the American flag was hoisted in front of millions.

I set out to jog a few miles the following day, and that was the end of my boxing career. I wanted to be in the final gold medal round without understanding the hard work, discipline, and committed practice it takes to achieve that level of success. So in my moment of pain, I quit.

I had no coach, no level of accountability, and no discipline. If I had, I might have gone beyond the first day of jogging. This is precisely why the coaching relationship is listed under the intensive level of mentoring. It requires significant effort.

Intensive Level Summary

The intensive level requires a higher degree of commitment, responsibility, and accountability from both mentors and mentorees. The intent is serious growth, maturity, and development. Disciplers work with new believers in developing the foundational skills necessary to follow Jesus. Mentorees are moved from dependence upon the mentor to healthy independence and self-motivated pursuit of God. Spiritual guides work with believers on such issues as maturity, commitment, motivation, integrity, accountability, direction, and how to address specific spiritual concerns. Mentorees are moved from independence to interdependence. Coaches work with mentorees to develop and sharpen specific skills and abilities in order to successfully complete a task or perform a new challenge.

OCCASSIONAL LEVEL

The occasional level is seated between the passive and intensive categories to indicate its middle-of-the-road status. Less deliberate than the previous level, it lacks the intense commitment and accountability factor; yet, it is far more structured than the passive level, which can be almost structure-less. Mentors in the occasional level perform one of three different roles (counselor, teacher, sponsor) that are highly advantageous to mentorees in their hour of special need.

While there is overlap and similarity between the various mentoring roles in the different levels, the *focus* of each style is the distinguishing factor. The counselor, for instance, focuses on offering timely advice and impartial perspectives regarding any number of issues and circumstances. This is much broader than the narrow emphasis of the spiritual guide in the intensive level. Our perspective is often biased or incorrect about a host of things, and counselors facilitate a healthy balance by placing our viewpoints on the table for critical examination. Listening to the advice and wisdom of a trusted counselor can be immensely beneficial.

Timely advice from someone who acts as a trusted counselor can be seen in the book of Exodus as Moses, someone with a specific need, receives counsel from his father-in-law, Jethro. The account is presented in Exodus 18:13–27:

It came about the next day that Moses sat to judge the people, and the people stood about Moses from the morning until the evening. Now when Moses' father-in-law saw all that he was doing for the people, he said, "What is this thing that you are doing for the people? Why do you alone sit as judge and all the people stand about you from morning until evening?" Moses said to his father-in-law, "Because the people come to me to inquire of God. When they have a dispute, it comes to me, and I judge between a man and his neighbor and make known the statutes of God and His laws."

Moses' father-in-law said to him, "The thing that you are doing is not good. You will surely wear out, both yourself and these people who are with you, for the task is too heavy for you; you cannot do it alone. Now listen to me: I will give you counsel, and God be with you. You be the people's representative before God, and you bring the disputes to God, then teach them the statutes and the laws, and make known to them the way in which they are to walk and the work they are to do. Furthermore, you shall select out of all the people able men who fear God, men of truth, those who hate dishonest gain; and you shall place these over them as leaders of thousands, of hundreds, of fifties and of tens. Let them judge the people at all times; and let it be that every major dispute they will bring to you, but every minor dispute they themselves will judge. So it will be easier for you, and they will bear the burden with you. If you do this thing and God so commands you, then you will be able to endure, and all these people also will go to their place in peace."

So Moses listened to his father-in-law and did all that he had said. Moses chose able men out of all Israel and made them heads over the people, leaders of thousands, of hundreds, of fifties and of tens. They judged the people at all times; the difficult dispute they would bring to Moses, but every minor dispute they themselves would judge. Then Moses bade his father-in-law farewell, and he went his way into his own land.

In this instance, Jethro notices a very specific lapse in Moses' leadership practice. Since an established relationship already exists, Jethro feels comfortable offering advice for the benefit of Moses and the people. Jethro's wise words are apropos since Moses faces extreme fatigue from judging all the people himself. If things don't change quickly, he will soon be overwhelmed, and the task will squash his ability to perform adequately. Moses listens and implements his father-in-law's sage advice. The counseling session is over, and Jethro moves on to other things. Counseling need not continue for long periods of time and may not contain the heavy accountability required of the intensive level. Short encounters like this one may provide timely assistance for specific circumstances.

The Bible speaks favorably of timely counsel, as seen in the following examples from Proverbs:

> **Proverbs 12:15**
> The way of a fool is right in his own eyes, but a wise man is he who listens to counsel.
>
> **Proverbs 15:22–23**
> Without consultation, plans are frustrated, but with many counselors they succeed. A man has joy in an apt answer, and how delightful is a timely word!
>
> **Proverbs 20:18**
> Prepare plans by consultation, and make war by wise guidance.

Personal pride or foolish stubbornness can hinder the receiving of advice from others, but ignoring trusted counsel is a costly mistake. Advice readily arises from peers and colleagues who understand each other's situations. Familiarity with the lingo, circumstances, possible outcomes, etc., allows them to offer perspective with understanding and empathy. Be careful though, for someone *too* close to the situation may be biased and offer skewed advice, whereas an outsider's impartiality may provide broader, unbiased viewpoints. Outsiders have nothing to gain except to provide sound counsel. When seeking advice, find someone who understands your context without being involved to the point of partiality.

In one particular church, younger women lamented the fact that there were no older ladies able to counsel them. On several occasions, these young ladies sought counsel from those more experienced; instead of advice, they received criticism. The older women probably had much to give, but lacked wisdom and tact in conveying it. They seemed much more interested in condemnation and conformity to personal preferences.

An elder in one of my former churches claimed to have the gift of discernment. His unbridled gift was so out of hand that he felt every decision of the governing board should go through him for approval. His gift of discernment, he reasoned, gave him the right to make all decisions. Though he desired to act as counselor, he simply alienated everyone with the inappropriate use of his self-proclaimed gift. While wanting to "discern" for everyone else, he was unable to "discern" for himself.

Not only must counselors possess the experience and knowledge necessary to act as advice-givers, they must also do so in a timely manner. Counseling mentors focus on offering timely and appropriate advice that helps mentorees navigate specific circumstances.

After many years in full-time ministry, I procured a respite at a Christian retreat center designed for members of the clergy. Professional, qualified counselors were available to anyone in need. The beautiful mountain chalet nestled in tranquility had no television to interrupt the day, and it was heavenly. I maximized my week by meeting with one of the counselors. It was a time to bounce off ideas, share ministry philosophies, check and balance my perspectives, and receive valuable counsel.

I was delighted to hit upon an impartial third party who could help me separate fact from fiction. During our first meeting, I said matter-of-factly, "I want to tell you where I've been, where I am now, and where I want to go. I value your input and ask you to honestly tell me if I'm on the right track or if there is something I am overlooking." Though taken aback by my directness, he knew I was serious, and by the end of the week said, "Usually I can't share too deeply with those who come here because they really don't want to hear it. But you are willing to hear the truth and are serious about putting it into action." I guess my note-taking during our sessions gave me away. His unbiased perspective was important to me. Even though we met for only two hours a day for several days, his timely and appropriate counsel came at just the right time and in the right manner.

The role of counselor can be either formal or informal. The degree of accountability varies depending upon the needs of mentorees. Sometimes mentors initiate timely advice if a strong relationship already exists, but typically mentorees sense a need and seek out appropriate individuals. The principle of attraction and an atmosphere of trust are conducive to the receiving of advice. The length of time spent with counselors is not as important as the timeliness and soundness of the counsel given.

Teacher

The occasional mentoring level also contains the role of teacher, whose primary focus is to impart knowledge and understanding regarding a specific subject. The sharing of such information empowers mentorees toward further growth and development.

I felt satisfaction upon completing my first furniture refinishing project. Working with wood was enjoyable. Soon, my interest grew to the point where a few power tools were required. Others had spoken of routers, so I sought to purchase one. While strolling through the hardware store one day, my attention was drawn to router tables. They looked interesting, but I couldn't figure out how they worked. It seemed as if there should be a place on top of the table for the router to sit. Instead, there was a big hole in the center of the table. Realizing my severe lack of knowledge on the subject, I asked a friend, known for his woodworking skills, to impart some knowledge to me.

One morning, he helped me understand how routers work. As it turns out, the router attaches to the table from the bottom. Duh! He taught me about router bits, woodworking safety, and how to operate the tool. He even brought over a stack of wood so I could practice. His sharing of detailed information provided me with a fresh ability to effectively use my new power tool.

I seek out individuals all the time who possess specific knowledge in the areas of growth I desire to pursue. I initiate contact, request their input for essential reading on the subject, and ask if I can take them out for lunch to dive deeper. Most are thrilled with the opportunity to impart their knowledge and experience with someone earnestly seeking to learn. These are great moments of enlightenment. The role of teacher can be incredibly formal with time commitments, clear expectations, and accountability, or informal—such as my experience with router knowledge that lasted only a few hours.

As part of my doctoral program, I developed and taught a theology course specifically designed for average church-goers. With a small group of participants, we began the first of twenty-five theological lessons. It was a formal gathering with pre- and post-testing. As the teacher, I was formally imparting knowledge to individuals desiring growth in their understanding of theology.

For the teaching role to occur, all you really need is 1) someone who possesses special knowledge and is willing to share that knowledge, and 2) someone who desires to learn what teachers are willing to share. The two of them get together, and one shares while the other learns. The duration of the relationship may be long or short depending on the mentoree's needs, the subject matter, and the level of mastery desired.

The term "teacher" should not be thought of as the stereotypical bow-tied professor communicating in boring, monotone fashion. Though most professors are not stereotypical, it is extremely important that they communicate effectively. Successful teachers exude enthusiasm for the subject matter, illustrate pertinent concepts, apply learning to real life, and motivate mentorees to pursue further learning. Quality teachers prepare well, organize their subject, connect learners with appropriate resources, effectively communicate, and provide evaluation to ensure that learning has occurred.

Learning is a continuous, life-long endeavor. With so many people possessing specialized knowledge in areas that we do not, it is wise to assume a learning posture. Knowledge areas are as varied as there are needs, and the key to finding a teaching mentor is to know exactly what it is you desire to learn. The better you specify your need, the easier it is to find someone who can provide the knowledge you seek.

Sponsor

The final task mentors might assume in the occasional level is the role of sponsor—someone who focuses on helping individuals move upward in their careers. Sponsors typically maintain higher positions of authority with greater resources and credibility to assist those lower on the career ladder. This could involve introducing mentorees to key influencers, making recommendations for advancement, serving as a confidante, offering navigational support within the labyrinthine organizational culture, and facilitating the making of significant contributions. Sponsors assist potential leaders with upward mobility.

This mentoring relationship is typically initiated by sponsors as they scan the horizon for individuals who possess an innate drive and desire to contribute. They look for those who show promise, can impact the organization, and will respond positively to their sponsoring oversight.

Sponsors understand the intricate organizational workings and maintain a network of indispensable relationships for career mobility. They can open doors and convince noteworthy individuals to give mentorees a chance at positions that challenge and reveal their abilities. As strategic people within organizations, sponsors desire what is best for both the individual and the organization. Good sponsors are devoid of self-seeking ambition and are willing to risk their own reputations.

Sponsors not only open doors, but they often create them. If necessary, they may establish new positions for mentorees, but they can also remove individuals from the organization if it is advantageous for everyone involved. The best career track may actually be outside the organization for some who are far ahead of where an organization is in its vision, goals, and capabilities, or when the organization is unable to provide the necessary challenges for those with exceptional potential and skill. To avoid personal frustration and possible organizational conflict, moving mentorees to another organization where their full potential is realized may be best. Though this move may sting for a bit, if done with honesty and compassion, it acts as a protective device guiding mentorees into more suitable situations.

This could easily be misconstrued as some slick power maneuver to rid organizations of those who might outshine the sponsor, and to be sure, these things do occur. Most sponsors, however, are well trained and serve in sponsoring roles because of their maturity and interest in both the organization and the mentoree.

Some argue that the sponsoring role leaves God out of the picture. But this need not be, and it is a grave mistake to think so. We can't just sit on the sofa and say, "God lead me," and never leave the couch, never talk to anyone, never increase our skills, and never do our part. It is difficult to drive a parked car. We are active participants in the *process* of following God, and so are others. God can use a sponsor to deeply impact the life of another. He oversees our life, moves and directs our affairs, and uses other people—including sponsors—to influence us.

God's actions don't occur in a vacuum. He uses people, circumstances, and events to move us from where we are to where He wants us to be. If someone in an organization recognizes potential within you, trains you, and brings you to a place of leadership and influence, the proper response is to recognize that it all came from the Creator's hand. Sponsors merely recognize what God has placed inside of you. The sponsor may be an instrument in the hand of God, and establishing sponsoring relationships could very well be the Lord's work in your life!

My entrance into Christian higher education came about in this manner. For several years, I sensed the Lord's leading in this direction, but appropriate openings never materialized. Finally, an academic dean noticed the promise within me and the benefit I could bring to his institution. The door opened wide, and a totally new career and ministry began. While it was the academic dean who turned the doorknob, it was the Lord who opened the door.

Any organization (including the church) that neglects to sponsor exceptional individuals and move them through the ranks is in danger of losing them through the back door. Many denominations have lost potential leaders to other churches, parachurch ministries, and even secular organizations because they were unable to provide sustaining challenges and opportunities. Organizations and churches must recognize this fact while identifying and releasing strategic sponsors who can develop mentorees. This benefits the organization, the individual, and the kingdom.

Occasional Level Summary

The occasional level of mentoring is nestled between the passive and intensive categories because it is much more structured and deliberate than the passive level, while lacking the heavy doses of commitment, responsibility, and accountability required of the intensive level. Its focus is upon helping mentorees in times of special need through three primary roles (counselor, teacher, sponsor).

Counselors focus on offering timely advice and impartial perspectives. The value of a trusted counselor cannot be overstated. Teachers focus on imparting specific knowledge and understanding with inspiration, excitement, and relevance. There are times when mentorees must acquire new knowledge and skills in order to move forward. Teachers do the teaching; mentorees do the learning. Without sponsors, many potential leaders would fall between the cracks. Sponsors focus on helping individuals move upward in their career or ministry for greater influence within the organization. It could be considered leadership development.

PASSIVE LEVEL

Of the three levels of mentoring, the passive level is the least deliberate and intensive. This category houses two mentoring roles: contemporary and historical. These roles are considered passive because there is no deliberate or direct relationship between the mentor and mentoree—one simply learns by reading or watching. Often, those being observed don't even know others are watching.

The contemporary model of mentoring is "contemporary" because it involves observing a *living* person in today's world. The historical model, on the other hand, involves learning from someone who is deceased, but who mentors through biographies, autobiographies, and other writings. It is considered "historical" because the individual is no longer living in the contemporary world.

Passive mentoring is a viable option for those lacking access to mentors. Due to circumstances or location, mentors may not be readily available. Living in a geographically secluded region, for instance, may diminish the chance of finding local mentors; there simply may not be enough competent or willing individuals in your area. Some may be unwilling to involve themselves in an occasional or intensive mentoring relationship due to fear. At this point in their lives, it is just too much for them. In these cases, passive mentoring takes on a new dimension of importance. Lest we conclude that passive mentoring is "less than" mentoring, we remember that everyone can be involved in this level. Its silent impact can be significant.

Since there is no direct relationship involved, mentorees must supply the needed dynamics for successful mentoring, even if it is only one-sided. How can the dynamic of attraction occur when the mentor may not even know of the situation? If you are drawn to the style of ministry, values, or written works of specific individuals, attraction is present. You can observe their every move or read every article they have written without that person ever knowing you exist. Attraction is present but is supplied solely by the mentoree.

Mentorees also supply the needed dynamic of responsiveness. Passive mentors cannot directly insist on better performance, spend time helping to grasp a concept, or evaluate progress. Responsiveness is determined solely by the mentoree. Similarly, the dynamic of accountability is low because the mentor is not personally requiring it. The contemporary and historical model of mentoring can be quite beneficial if mentorees provide the necessary dynamics for growth and development.

Contemporary mentoring involves modeling, and modeling is a biblical concept. Peter exhorts the elders in local congregations to be examples to their flock: "shepherd the flock of God among you, exercising oversight not under compulsion, but voluntarily, according to the will of God; and not for sordid gain, but with eagerness; nor yet as lording it over those allotted to your charge, but proving to be examples to the flock" (I Pt. 5:2–3). Jesus is also said to be an example for us, as seen in the following verses:

> **1 Peter 2:21**
> For you have been called for this purpose, since Christ also suffered for you, leaving you an example for you to follow in His steps.
>
> **1 John 2:6**
> The one who says he abides in Him ought himself to walk in the same manner as He walked.
>
> **John 13:14–15**
> If I then, the Lord and the Teacher, washed your feet, you also ought to wash one another's feet. For I gave you an example that you also should do as I did to you.

Because Paul modeled his life after Jesus, he could confidently advise the Corinthians:

1 Corinthians 4:16–17
Therefore I exhort you, therefore, be imitators of me. For this reason I have sent to you Timothy, who is my beloved and faithful child in the Lord, and he will remind you of my ways which are in Christ, just as I teach everywhere in every church.

Likewise, Paul instructs the Philippian church:

Philippians 4:9
The things you have learned and received and heard and seen in me, practice these things, and the God of peace will be with you.

Modeling extends to virtually every arena of life. Supervisors model attitudes and behaviors to their employees that shape the work environment. Parents, whether they like to admit it or not, model all kinds of things to their children who, both consciously and unconsciously, emulate what they see. Holding high positions of leadership and influence, pastors and elders not only become models for the congregation, but congregations often reflect what is occurring in the circle of leadership.

One obvious aspect of contemporary modeling is the reality that anyone can watch and observe. Individuals can be positively challenged by the powerful example of another. Though living examples are far from perfect, they embody values, attitudes, and behaviors that may be worth emulating. We must realize that others are watching us and that our lives can become powerful demonstrations of what it means to live by faith. By observing and emulating living models, mentorees take big steps forward in their own development. Since historical mentors are no longer living, they model through the pages of a book. Modeling ensues from what is read, rather than actual observation.

Years ago, I received a paperback on the life of George Mueller who lived in the 1800s and oversaw an orphanage. As I read the book, I was amazed at this man's simple faith. When a financial, personal, or physical need arose, he simply looked to God with faithful resolve. I love his story because he is a powerful example to me of absolute trust in God.

Deitrich Bonhoeffer's book *The Cost of Discipleship* also mentored me with tremendous affect. Bonhoeffer contrasts cheap grace with costly grace and it struck me hard. One quote in particular left its deep impression upon my soul: "When Christ calls a man, He bids him come and die." Although he didn't survive WWII, Bonhoeffer embodied a perspective that changed my life and helped me reflect upon the true cost of being a Christian.

While working on my graduate degree in theology, I fondly remember the "flame room" in the library basement. The prayer bench in the middle of the room was surrounded by biographies, autobiographies, and classic writings of wise men and women of faith. Though long gone, the seminary recognized the continuing impact these individuals still have upon modern-day readers.

Passive mentoring is a wonderful way of growing and learning for those unable or unwilling to establish a direct and deliberate mentoring relationship. It is also a complimentary side dish for those already involved in the occasional or intensive mentoring levels. The passive category allows everyone to be involved. Even you.

9

PRACTICAL HELPS

BALANCED RELATIONSHIPS

As with most things in life, balance is essential to maintaining positive health and a sense of wellbeing. When our equilibrium is out of sorts, we become like wobbly washing machines spinning wildly out of control. Too much emphasis on exercise without proper nutrition, for instance, creates imbalance. Too much ministry activity without adequate family time creates imbalance. Too much emphasis on love without the proper balancing of truth brings about distortion. Too much emphasis on tradition can push away new ideas. Balance is essential in virtually every arena of life, and mentoring relationships are no exception.

Christians earnestly seek to make their life count for the kingdom and, in some way, become a catalyst for change in others. My sister sang a touching song at the funeral of a beloved friend while the thoughts of many were focused upon human mortality. An indelible impression was cast upon me with the phrase, "Only one life twill soon be past, only what's done for Christ will last." Wrapped in that little phrase is a truth worth pondering. We want our lives to count for something, possess meaning, and significantly impact others rather than building on precarious foundations of wood, hay, and stubble (1 Cor. 3:12–14). If we look forward to the day when we stand before our Creator and receive His approval for a life well lived (1 Cor. 4:5), it is essential that we surround ourselves with relational networks of accountability. We become isolated if we don't, and isolation increases the odds of failure.

Paul maintained a relational network of accountability in his own life. Gamaliel and Barnabas are mentors. Timothy and Titus are mentorees. Numerous colleagues become peer ministry partners. Paul does not isolate himself. Until the end, he surrounds himself with mentors, mentorees, and peers. He writes letters, pursues personal visits, and shares with each of those in his network of accountability. This relational balance enhances his ministry and his relationship with God and others.

There are three dimensions to a balanced network of relational accountability: Up, down, and sideways. [17] Relationships in each direction help maintain balance in our lives.

Upward Dimension

The upward dimension involves being mentored by someone who has more experience, knowledge, and wisdom than you. There will never be a time when we do not need to involve ourselves in continual development. Realizing this, we willingly place ourselves in mentoring relationships. Maintaining a teachable spirit throughout life is essential for growth. Believing we have reached the pinnacle of knowledge is merely climbing the mountain of self-deceit. We are "aliens and strangers" on this planet in a continual process of becoming more like Jesus.

RELATIONAL NETWORK OF ACCOUNTABILITY

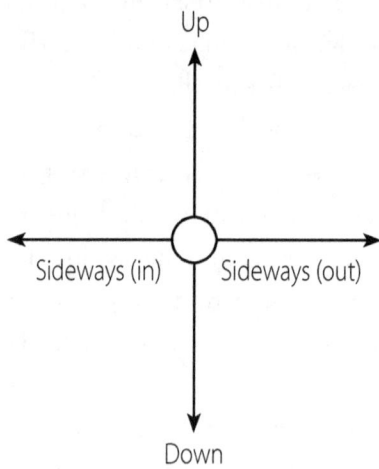

Lifelong learning is a habit of the mind that aids our diverse learning needs throughout life's transitions. Early on in ministry, for instance, individuals may require mentors who provide perspective, support, and insight into new surroundings not yet experienced. As one grows older, the need may be for more reflection, understanding complex processes, grasping a bigger picture, or contemplating the future. Mentors are valuable at every juncture in life.

Since locating perfect individuals who can mentor *everything* isn't going to happen, mentorees must understand the area in which they need to grow. As a practical matter, this leaves room for mentors to accept several mentorees. Everyone can mentor someone in *something*. Connecting what you know with someone who needs that knowledge can transform a life. Stories abound of past drug addicts, prostitutes, and alcoholics who invest their lives to serve others who are currently where they once were. They simply help others as they themselves have been helped. The stories, however, need not be so dramatic. Beth, for example, has never been involved with drugs, prostitution, or alcoholism, and desires to be an exemplary Sunday School teacher inspiring children the way her Sunday School teacher inspired her. She discovers a teacher willing to invest in her and a mentoring relationship is inaugurated.

Downward Dimension

Not only do upward mentors help *us* continue the process of growth, but mentoring someone below (downward) helps *others* in their maturation process. Investing our life, experience, and knowledge in others is a fruitful and meaningful endeavor. Instilling commitment, values, and understanding moves the next generation to faithfully carry on the meaning and message of Christianity.

Investing what you have in others is downward mentoring. Downward mentoring doesn't equate to a master-servant relationship where the one on top controls the one on the bottom. Actually, the terms "upward" and "downward" have nothing to do with lording over others. Power and control is not the process by which mentoring is accomplished. Upward and downward are merely useful terms describing whether you are being mentored (upward) or are mentoring another (downward). The potential result of downward mentoring is to mark other human beings in such a way that they become better and stronger. Helping others succeed can bring relational balance to our life.

Horizontal Dimension

The horizontal dimension involves balancing our relationships with peers who are on the same level. Colleagues naturally possess similarities that allow for sharing, comparing notes on related circumstances, sharpening each other, and gathering support and insight. It is wonderful to share with others who have been there before (upward) or someone who will someday be there (downward), but life can be pretty lonely without someone who is there right now, alongside of you (peer). Peers can encourage perseverance.

Women tend to have more peer relationships than men, but all relationships that exhibit high levels of trust and commitment bring greater relational balance. As a leader, you need someone other than your spouse on a peer level. Claiming hundreds of acquaintances is easy, but often there are very few close friends with whom leaders can share openly and honestly. It has been suggested that peer relationships involve someone from within your church or organization as well as someone from the outside. This way, you receive benefit from both perspectives.

Sometimes peer relationships within the church occur in small groups such as a men's prayer group or couples' Bible study. While this may be a lush environment for peer relationships, there is a down side to keep in mind. When groups contain too many people, or the wrong mix of people, the depth of sharing can be inhibited and accountability falls by the wayside. Groups are usually unable to reach the depth of a one-on-one relationship.

David and Jonathan's relationship in I Samuel is a prime example of a close peer friendship. Both are proven warriors. David kills the giant Goliath, and Jonathan heroically faces the Philistines on the outskirts of Gibeah. They are about the same age, and both are leaders. They experience the same environment in the house and army of Saul. They are committed to each other through a sworn friendship in the name of the Lord. They mutually encourage and sharpen one another, placing each other's best interest ahead of their own.

Ecclesiastes 4:9–10 addresses the positive benefits of the friendship factor:

> Two are better than one because they have a good return for their labor. For if either of them falls, the one will lift up his companion. But woe to the one who falls when there is not another to lift him up.

A relationally balanced network is extremely beneficial. We all need mentors over us (upward) to assist us in sailing the uncharted waters of life. We all need mentorees under us (downward) in whom we can invest our life, enabling them to serve the Lord faithfully and effectively. Finally, we need peers who share common interests, understandings, and familiarities with whom we can experience honest sharing, mutual encouragement, and loving accountability.

LEARNING FROM OUR PREDECESSORS

Many have involved themselves in mentoring relationships long before we ever decided to attach a label to it as a worthy and fruitful endeavor. We can learn from the successes and failures of those who have walked the path before us. What follows is a brief listing of relevant points on establishing mentoring relationships garnered from those who have journeyed before us.

1. Establish and develop the relationship.

As simple as it sounds, mentoring does not occur without the existence of a relationship. Since mentoring takes place within a relational environment, this aspect is foundational. Sometimes mentoring relationships develop naturally, and at other times a more deliberate effort is needed. The stronger the relationship, the greater potential there is for growth and development. Better results are attained with strong relational bonds. Establishing and developing the relationship is important, for without it, mentoring merely becomes a sterile experience.

2. Mutually agree on the goals of the relationship.

The lack of clear goals and expectations on the part of both parties is one of the biggest reasons that mentoring can be frustrating. Discussing this element is embarrassing for many because they fear it could be perceived as too pushy and possibly jeopardize the relationship. This, of course, is contrary to what really happens.

When goals and expectations are clearly expressed and agreed upon, the parties know their role in the relationship. Without this, how do we know if goals have been attained? How do we know if our responsibility is adequately being fulfilled? A relationship with no purpose, unclear goals, and little expectation is doomed for failure. Clear markers allow everyone to know where they are and where they need to go, and in the intensive mentoring level, this is often negotiated at the outset. When mentorees and mentors share their needs, expectations, and goals, they can agree on the best path forward. At other times, goals and expectations are expressed in gentler terms. Nonetheless, relationships are enhanced when there is clarity around mentoring goals.

3. Agree upon a meeting schedule.

Many relationships require weekly meetings and some monthly meetings, while others meet as they are able. It is helpful to agree upon the frequency of getting together. Consider each other's schedules and the purpose of the relationship. Depending on need, some relationships may require longer and more frequent meetings than others. Will your meetings be face-to-face, phone conversations, or online discussions? Will the mentor be available for impromptu meetings outside of the regular schedule? Be sure to also address the issue of emergency meetings in times of crisis.

4. Agree upon a method and structure of accountability.

Repetition is an effective reminder, so I will say it again: people tend to do what we inspect, not what we expect. In order to achieve the goals and expectations mutually agreed upon, accountability provides both the mentor and mentoree with a mechanism for monitoring and measuring tasks and achievements. Accountability is the conduit for evaluating progress and determining what remains to be accomplished in moving forward.

What will be the method and structure of accountability? Will it be informal mentoring with little accountability or formal structures that include such things as written assignments, required readings, formal and informal assessments, phone calls, times for discussion and questions, etc? Be sure to discuss the accountability factor and agree upon how it will be achieved.

5. Discuss the concept of confidentiality.

A sure way for ministers to lose congregational trust is to preach on Sunday morning what was shared with them in private throughout the week. Wise ministers realize that a breach of confidentiality negatively impacts ministry effectiveness. Confidentiality is a must, especially in relationships where open and honest sharing is expected. Individuals don't want to share deeply only to have their innermost self exposed to the rest of the world. Some individuals are private and reserved, while others could care less who knows what about them. Yet, without confidentiality, there will be little honest communication. Clarify confidentiality expectations and preclude problems before they arise.

6. Set a time frame upon the relationship.
Mentoring relationships don't always last forever, nor are they expected to. Relational time frames revolve around the needs and goals of the mentoree, and establishing various intervals for evaluating the relationship is beneficial. If you believe it will take a year for the relationship to accomplish its intended purpose, agree upon a one-year time frame with quarterly intervals of evaluation. This way, if things are not going smoothly, the relationship can be shut down during an evaluation period instead of enduring a negative experience for an entire year. This allows either party to back away without hurt feelings. These evaluation periods also allow for modifications to the original expectations and goals. Be sure to ask mentorees for feedback. Is the relationship scratching where they are itching?

Without bringing closure to the relationship, the quality of mentoring dwindles and both parties become uneasy about what to do next. The key to overcoming this potential obstacle is to discuss the end at the beginning. When the initial time frame is up, both mentor and mentoree may decide to extend the arrangement, but it is always best to confer up front how and when you will end the mentoring relationship. When the agreed-upon timeframe is over, a close enough relationship often exists for occasional mentoring to continue.

EVERYDAY ARENAS FOR MENTORING
The Family
It is possible for mentoring to occur on a regular basis within common, everyday arenas of life. Key contexts for such relationships may be surprising, since they can be so routine and familiar. One of the most important and well-known environments for mentoring is found in the home. Right before our

very eyes lie valuable mentoring opportunities within the mix of fathers, mothers, grandparents, and children.

The family unit is an exceptional environment for mentoring because relational networks are already in place. Everyone is together as a family unit, a perfect atmosphere for mentoring.

Husbands and wives can mentor each other as well as their children. In one sense, mentoring occurs in this situation, no matter what, because of existing relationships and proximity of family members. Being aware of your natural mentoring environment can help you model positive behaviors, attitudes, and values. Spouses can discuss what they learn from one another, both good and bad, in an effort toward helping one another grow.

Sarah was brought up to always do what people expected since disappointing others was unacceptable. Her behavioral motivation was to meet the demands and expectations of others while dropping her own needs along the wayside.

On several occasions, Sarah attests to her husband's influence in this area of her life. He modeled appropriate behavior and helped her reason through a flawed belief system. She has since learned to relax and do what God alone expects. She is still as nice and helpful as ever, but she now engages in acts of kindness with the right motivation. This has taken significant courage on her part as the expectations of some are outrageous and ridiculous. Her husband's modeling freed her from the heavy bondage of others' expectations and released her for effective ministry in the area of God's calling.

Sarah has mentored her husband, Martin, as well. Sarah has a gentle and caring demeanor that makes others feel comfortable in her presence. Her kindness and grace pleasantly disarms friends and strangers. Martin remembers visiting a nursing home while they were dating. Sarah brought chocolates to several ladies she had "adopted" on a volunteer basis. Her disarming nature, modeled throughout the years, has helped Martin become more caring and gracious. There are many ways, both big and small, in which Sarah and Martin have mentored one another.

Proverbs 22:6 states, "Train up a child in the way he should go, even when he is old he will not depart from it." Mentoring is an important way to train children. The home provides a wonderful context for modeling kingdom values to our children and what it means to love God and others with all our heart. Though children may feign disinterest, they are indeed watching whether our conduct matches our speech. The home front, a routine and familiar place, can be a natural environment for family mentoring.

The Church

The local church is another routine setting for productive mentoring. While we know that pastors hold important positions of influence, we may not fully grasp just how much they possess. Pastors and church leaders know from firsthand experience that their behaviors and attitudes communicate to others around them. Leadership positions bring with it the role of example-setter. Being a pastor involves far more than merely preaching a sermon on Sunday morning. I have read that approximately seventy-five percent of all American churches are under one hundred people and ninety percent are under 350 parishioners. This means that highly relational contexts are the norm for pastors.

Anyone in the congregation can be involved in mentoring as long as they are willing to share their God-given resources. How one supports the church, responds to the teaching and preaching of Scripture, displays a positive attitude toward leadership, serves in ministry roles, etc., all convey messages to others. Dropping the kids off for Sunday School while mom and dad go out for coffee communicates disinterest. Falling asleep during the morning service rarely inspires others. When relationships within the church are positive and healthy, others are stirred toward a deeper walk with the Lord. The example of another can be just the type of timely inspiration needed to complete a task or motivate another to further service.

I will never forget the inspirational speaker who spoke during a morning church service. His message led to the congregation holding hands in a large circle while the pastor closed in prayer. As a teenager, I meticulously observed this guest speaker who had so eloquently unlocked the mysteries of the Bible. During our time of prayer, he glanced at his watch several times, and this disgusted me. In typical teenager judgmentalism, I thought to myself, "This guy is more concerned with getting out of here than with the wonderful response he received from the people." The wind was taken from my sail, and his eloquent address suddenly lost all credibility.

On a positive note, I know of no one who more closely resembles Jesus than my former pastor. As a young boy, I watched him. As a college student, I watched him. As an adult, I still have my eye on him, for he is the epitome of what I want to be and how I desire to live for God. His devout behavior and my watchful eyes connected within the context of the church to powerfully influence my life. The local assembly can become a marvelous environment for influencing others.

Books

One special mentoring context for me has been the reading of books. I realize this subject has already been broached under the passive level of mentoring, but reading has had such a powerful impact upon me that I want to emphasize the topic.

For Christmas one year, my wife and I agreed on a specified sum of money for each of us to purchase reading material. We carefully selected the books and gleefully opened the boxes containing our Christmas presents to one another. To my great joy, it was one of the best Christmas gifts I have ever received. We want to do it again.

Words cannot describe how often I have been motivated and inspired by reading the works of others. My frequent writing today, I suspect, stems from the impact books have played in my own growth. In my study, I often break down into tears of confession, loud singing, and thanksgiving prayers for a new truth learned or a story that touched my heart. If you are not a reader, may I encourage you to spend time with books? While the distinguished philosopher Dr. Elton Trueblood was showing me around his beautiful library on the campus of Earlham College, he said, "It's not the number of books you have but the quality of books that count." Acquire good books, ones that can be read again and again for continual development and inspiration.

10

EXPANDING THE BLESSING

MENTORING WITHIN THE CHURCH

If mentoring is a relational model worthy of our attention, how can we expand its blessings to those within our congregations? One summer day, several young ladies in the church approached me with a concern after reading Titus 2:3–5:

> Older women likewise are to be reverent in their behavior, not malicious gossips nor enslaved to much wine, teaching what is good, so that they may encourage the young women to love their husbands, to love their children, to be sensible, pure, workers at home, kind, being subject to their own husbands, so that the word of God will not be dishonored.

With a genuine and sensitive spirit, these young ladies asked why Titus 2:3–5 wasn't occurring in our local assembly. They yearned for training, encouragement, and teaching from older women. Sadly enough, as they looked around the congregation, they were unable to identify one woman who was both willing and capable of handling such a task. As I examined the church roster, I realized they had a good point. If our older ladies were given the chance, most would seize the mentoring opportunity to chastise the younger women for all the things they should be doing. Most of their "coulda, shoulda, oughta" items revolved around personal preferences rather than biblical mandates. Unfortunately, they would spend the majority of their time majoring on the minors with disastrous results.

This true scenario reveals the lack of positive mentoring relationships in the average church. The problem, I believe, lies not in the lack of potential mentorees, but in the lack of mentors who understand their role. In the previous example, there were plenty of ladies yearning to be mentorees, but not many positive mentors who understood their role and task.

When leaders grasp the enabling power of relationships they are often frustrated with how to implement mentoring on a wider basis. How can pastors expand mentoring beyond themselves so it takes on a greater role within the church body? There are no magical three-step formulas, and instead of using a fine brush for painting extreme detail, I share broad strokes that each church can implement in its own detailed manner.

Disseminate Information

The first broad brush stroke for expanding mentoring relationships is the dissemination of information. It is difficult to read the mind of others and then behave as they think you should. People respond best when given adequate information and plenty of time to chew on the matter.

Preaching on the subject of mentoring is one method for reaching the congregation. After all, it *is* a biblical topic. It *is* something that will impact the lives of congregational members. Design a catchy title and preach a series of messages accompanied with outlines for taking notes. This is one method of disseminating information to others within the local church.

Congregations often reflect what occurs in leadership, so it is wise to share information with church leaders. Help them understand and support the importance of mentoring. The elder or deacon board can read books together. Elders in my churches always read an agreed-upon book or two during the year and utilized an evening of fellowship, apart from regularly scheduled meeting times, to discuss its impact and importance.

Create an atmosphere where thorough discussion of the book can occur. To help leaders prepare for this evening, draft several questions ahead of time for consideration. For instance, when passing out the books, include a study sheet with several questions: What is the author's main point? This helps them to grasp the large picture. What points were most important for you and why? They don't have to choose points *you* feel are important; they answer from their perspective. What weaknesses do you see with the author's understanding of the material? Just because a book has been written doesn't mean authors have covered everything, or their arguments are valid and biblically sound. This allows readers to disagree or bring up issues not adequately addressed in the material.

Finally, you may want to ask personal questions. How has reading this book influenced you? How does this book affect our church? Are there things we need to change, address, or adopt in light of our reading? You might hear a leader say something like, "We really need to get our folks involved in these types of relationships. I didn't realize how important and powerful mentoring could be. How can our people become more relationally involved?" This opens the door for positive discussion regarding ways and means of implementation.

Other avenues of disseminating information might be to use the book in a Sunday School class, small group gathering, or retreat setting. I began a ministry within our church to avid book readers called "Book of the Every Other Month Club." Six times a year, this group met for coffee and discussion regarding relevant and pertinent writings. It became a valuable method for disseminating information within a relational setting. The books do the teaching. There are many ways to disseminate information. Be creative! Access to information helps individuals understand, process, respond, and implement new learning into their lives.

Modeling

Another way to expand mentoring beyond ourselves is through modeling. It is possible and even desirable, to be both a mentor and mentoree at the same time. This allows us to model continuous learning in our life while investing in others at the same time. Obviously, we are not referring to the sharing of privileged information and items of confidentiality, but you can always share what you are learning and how the relationship is impacting you. This opens doors for guiding others into mentoring relationships.

Encouraging and maintaining a learning posture within the church helps to expand the mentoring concept. An atmosphere of expectant learning is primed for mentoring relationships. Intellectually speaking, most congregations mentally assent to the need for continual growth. Experientially, however, they are about as open to growth as the White House is to an intruder. I know of congregations where doctrine is memorized verse by verse, but in the lives of the parishioners, there is a closing of spirits to one another. When churches corporately say, "God, we're not where you want us to be. Would You please help us maintain soft and teachable hearts that seek to know You more fully and in deeper ways?" This type of collective attitude is conducive to the flourishing of mentoring relationships.

Renewed interest at the denominational level is another way of modeling within the religious milieu. Many denominations assign mentors to rookie pastors in an effort to support them during those precarious first few years of ministry. These endeavors reveal the heartfelt need for expanding mentoring to a wider audience.

A Relationship, Not a Program

We often begin the initiation of a new ministry by shopping the market for a program. We do this for evangelistic efforts, Sunday School curriculum, summer children's ministries, and other areas. Since mentoring is relational, it is not an event or a program, but a process for enriching the lives of others. It is not a one-time activity, such as the annual Sunday school teacher appreciation banquet; it is something that lasts longer, takes more time, and is actively pursued by those who enjoy investing in others.

Small groups are very important within the church and sometimes are seen as the cure-all for the church's ills. While groups can talk about mentoring and help to establish mentoring, they are not mentoring. Mentoring is typically a one-on-one relationship, and we are wise not to confuse it with small group ministry.

In his book *Mentoring*, Bob Biehl lists several steps for launching a mentoring program within the church: [18]

1. *Brief your pastor and the board first.*
2. *Appoint a champion.*
3. *Establish a steering committee of people interested in mentoring.*
4. *Develop a list of members who would like to have a mentor.*
5. *Have an intergenerational retreat.*

6. Introduce mentoring to special groups in the church.

7. Have a mentor-protégé retreat.

8. Train and encourage mentors.

FINISHING THE RACE

An examination of mentoring would not be complete without discussing how to maintain strong moorings during the rough storms of life. Many of us begin the journey with high aspirations and the best of intentions. Yet, why do so many of us fail? Why do so many of us start the race, only to stumble, quit, and never cross the finish line?

The Bible discusses this very issue in several passages. The parable of the sower in Matthew 13:1–23 describes seed falling on various types of soils. Only the seed falling on good soil yields crops of one hundred, sixty, and thirty-fold. Of all the seed falling on the ground, only a minority produce fruit. In Matthew 7:21, Jesus clearly states that "Not everyone who says to me, 'Lord, Lord' will enter the kingdom of heaven, but he who does the will of my Father who is in heaven." Matthew 7:13–14 goes on to say, "Enter through the narrow gate; for the gate is wide and the way is broad that leads to destruction, and there are many who enter through it. For the gate is small and the way is narrow that leads to life, and there are few who find it." One thing is for sure—not everyone who begins the race will finish; not everyone who claims to follow Jesus actually knows Him.

Paul reveals his own intense desire to finish the race of life in Acts 20:24: "But I do not consider my life of any account as dear to myself, so that I may finish my course and the ministry which I received from the Lord Jesus, to testify solemnly of the gospel of the grace of God." He also challenges the Corinthian believers in 1 Corinthians 9:24–26:

> Do you not know that those who run in a race all run, but only one receives the prize? Run in such a way that you may win. Everyone who competes in the games exercises self-control in all things. They then do it to receive a perishable wreath, but we an imperishable. Therefore I run in such a way, as not without aim; I box in such a way, as not beating the air; but I discipline my body and make it my slave, so that, after I have preached to others, I myself will not be disqualified.

Clearly, Paul views this life as a race that involves hard work and self-discipline. The prize for completing the race is worthy of the effort. Near the end of his life, Paul states the following in 2 Timothy 4:6–8:

> For I am already being poured out as a drink offering, and the time of my departure has come. I have fought the good fight, I have finished the course, I have kept the faith; in the future there is laid up for me the crown of righteousness, which the Lord, the righteous Judge, will award to me on that day; and not only to me, but also to all who have loved His appearing.

Whether it's a race metaphor from Paul or a seed metaphor from Jesus, the Bible clearly understands that many will drop out. How do we ensure a finish line crossing in our life? Are there practical guidelines and suggestions for completing the race?

There are many biblical guideposts such as studying Scripture, being filled with the Holy Spirit, not allowing bitterness to take root in our lives, and so on. Living life without the foundation of Scripture is like building a house on sand. Sooner or later, the waves wash the foundation away and the house breaks apart while tumbling into the sea. Ascertaining biblical principles for living a God-pleasing life can become a familiar and well-practiced routine for every believer. In addition to strong scriptural moorings, there are additional characteristics of those who persevere to the end.

I remember watching a television documentary some years ago on the stressful life of chief executive officers (CEOs). Some interesting lessons were brought to light. Having heard for years that many don't last long in key leadership roles because of stress, this particular documentary considered if there were perfectly healthy CEOs despite their overloaded environment. Their discoveries were thought-provoking.

A large portion of the CEOs studied became physically ill under the stress of their jobs, and a small percentage actually died. The researchers also found a small group (7%) who were quite healthy despite the heavy exposure of stress. In many ways, this is similar to the biblical notion of many dropping out of the race. How did the seven percent stay the course?

Three Prevailing Attitudes

Researchers discovered three prevailing attitudes in healthy executives that were absent in non-healthy executives.

1. *View obstacles as challenges instead of threats.*
2. *Pursue commitment instead of denial.*
3. *Pursue control rather than hopelessness.*

View Obstacles as Challenges Instead of Threats

When glitches surfaced within the organization, even major hiccups, healthy CEOs saw them as problems to be solved rather than obstacles that would crush them. This difference in attitude meant being able to deal with issues in a constructive manner rather than being run over by them.

Pursue Commitment Instead of Denial

When difficulties arose, healthy executives did not deny their existence or sweep problems under the rug, as many organizations and churches do. Instead, they committed themselves, both internally and externally, to conquering the problem. Denying problems is to stick your head in the sand while your backside is exposed. To commit oneself internally refers to a mental determination to tackle problems. External commitment refers to actions and behaviors that actually do something about the matter. One without the other is fruitless. Healthy CEOs pursue commitment instead of denial.

Pursue Control Rather Than Hopelessness

Healthy executives maintain a certain level of control in dealing with setbacks. They do not manipulate people but orchestrate problem-solving strategies. If the obstacle is out of their league, they find others who can help. Crisis situations can develop when circumstances are viewed as hopeless. Healthy executives orchestrate solutions because they operate from calm control rather than dim despair. This attitude takes on special significance for believers when they realize God's involvement in the process. There is no need for hopelessness when God is ever present with us.

It is easy to see how these three attitudes provide positive, action-oriented outlooks rather than negative perspectives that collapse in difficult situations. How individuals view circumstances and events reveals a great deal regarding their success in life. Do you see the glass as half empty or half full? My wife's grandmother loved gardening and potted plants could be found throughout her house. During Christmas, one of the relatives gifted her several large bags of potting soil and bird seed. She responded by saying, "Terry, can you believe they gave me a sack of dirt for Christmas? How rude!" What was intended to be a thoughtful gift was viewed as a rude gesture, and it ruined her attitude toward the givers. Our attitude and perspective has much to do with whether we successfully finish the race despite the obstacles littering our path. Pursue control rather than helplessness.

Laughing at Ourselves

In additional to the three prevailing attitudes described above, other key items came into focus for the vigorous executives. Researchers discovered that maintaining a good sense of humor during times of stress was also present in healthy CEOs. Executives who flourished did not put others down; instead, they were able to laugh at themselves, their mistakes, and even used their humorous faults as a way of teaching others. Their life didn't fall apart with personal or professional imperfections. They laughed at their flaws, learned from them, and kept on going.

Leisure Activities

Researchers also determined that healthy executives made time for leisure activities despite stress overloads. They worked hard, but they also played hard. Exercise drains off stress. By maintaining leisure and exercise programs in their life they were able to deflect some of the negative aspects of stress.

Social Support System

Finally, the study found that healthy executives maintained strong social support systems. From a professional standpoint, colleagues are often a stronger network than family because so much time is spent in the work environment.

This in no way diminishes the role and importance of family, but it does show the need for social support systems that help us cope and maintain balance in stressful leadership positions.

Application to the Spiritual Realm

In applying these lessons to the spiritual realm, we first ask ourselves if we view obstacles as threats or challenges. Individuals who disagree with us, stand in our path, and block our efforts are most often viewed as obstacles. Disagreement can be healthy for churches because they have to work out their differences. Finding mutually agreeable solutions is an empowering process. If handled correctly, problem-solving becomes a bonding adventure.

Most people don't mind someone disagreeing with them because they realize differing opinions can bring clarification and eventually a better solution. What they do mind is *how* someone disagrees. Bitterness, blaming, shaming, and backbiting only add fuel to the fire. Antagonists are in every church, and it is their nature to destroy. They quickly suck the life out of others and make ministry a miserable experience instead of a spiritually growing endeavor. There is a difference between a difficult person and an antagonist. We are all difficult to someone at some time in our lives. You can work with difficult people, and while it is challenging, it is not impossible. Antagonists, however, are destructive and are affectionately referred to as "well-intentioned dragons." For this obstacle, you need a protective group surrounding you. Pastors, for instance, need a supportive leadership board to insulate them from the destructive effects of these fire-breathing dragons.

Generally, when people are viewed as challenges instead of threats, dialogue is more likely to occur. People are at various levels of spiritual maturity within the church family; there are babies, adolescents, young adults, mature individuals, and wise saints within the congregation. None of this has much to do with age, for I have met some very old babies and some very young, wise saints.

When potentially damaging obstacles arise in relationships, it is never healthy to deny their existence or sweep them under the rug. Jesus' entire lifestyle and ministry consisted of truth-telling in love rather than peace-keeping at all costs. Denying problems actually weakens relationships, while truth-telling in love strengthens them. Following the example of Jesus involves handling issues with truth and love while calling for a higher relational standard. Though difficult to do at times, it is always right to commit ourselves in thought and deed to working through relational issues. In doing so, we feel better about ourselves and the relationship knowing we did the right thing. The end result is often a durable relationship able to weather the test of time.

We find Jesus overcoming obstacles in Scripture by orchestrating their solutions. He doesn't leave people in hopeless situations; He works to provide answers. Jesus never uses or manipulates people; instead, He unearths solutions to their problems. If the first two attitudes are in place (viewing obstacles as challenges and pursuing commitment rather than denial), the third attitude falls into line (emphasizing control rather than hopelessness). If obstacles are viewed as challenges instead of threats, and if we are willing to deal with issues instead of sweeping them under the rug, we are more inclined to utilize problem-solving strategies instead of allowing hopelessness to set off the panic alarm.

As with any relationship, there are bound to be trials, disappointments, mistakes, and letdowns. We cannot control what others think or how they will respond in any given situation. In the process of becoming more like our Lord, it pays to remember that maturity is a process involving time and effort. Though perfection is simply unattainable in this life, we can learn from our blunders, relax a bit, laugh at ourselves, and enjoy life to the fullest. This is beneficial for our physical and spiritual health.

There are additional aspects of running the race that I have found extremely beneficial in my own life, and I want to share them with you.

Communion With God

The power to minister effectively and live positively stems primarily from within a person rather than from external actions. It is entirely possible, as the Pharisees prove, to perform outward religious acts with no inner connection to God. Jesus condemns such external focus. God has been, and always will be, concerned with the internal well-being of humankind. Anointing one of Jesse's sons as king of Israel, the Lord's choice is based on the heart rather than outward appearance. We read the following in I Samuel 16:7:

> But the Lord said to Samuel, "Do not look at his appearance or at the height of his stature, because I have rejected him; for God sees not as man sees, for man looks at the outward appearance, but the Lord looks at the heart."

Proverbs 4:23 instructs, "Watch over your heart with all diligence, for from it flow the springs of life." According to Jesus, the greatest commandment in Matthew 22:37 is to "Love the Lord your God with all your heart, and with all your soul, and with all your mind." Our heart, soul, and mind are internal facets of our being. When the internal aspects of our life are immersed in intimate communion with God, we are spiritually alive. Realizing the importance of the inner man, Paul actually prays for this kind of intimacy in Ephesians 3:14–21:

> For this reason I bow my knees before the Father, from whom every family in heaven and on earth derives its name, that He would grant you, according to the riches of His glory, to be strengthened with power through His Spirit in the inner man, so that Christ may dwell in your hearts through faith; and that you, being rooted and grounded in love, may be able to comprehend with all the saints what is the breadth and length and height and depth, and to know the love of Christ which surpasses knowledge, that you may be filled up to all the fullness of God.
>
> Now to Him who is able to do far more abundantly beyond all that we ask or think, according to the power that works within us, to Him be the glory in the church and in Christ Jesus to all generations forever and ever. Amen.

The Holy Spirit, who indwells every believer, mediates the presence of Jesus within us. This is one of His important roles. He is able to strengthen the inner aspects of our lives. We know many individuals who are unimpressive on the outside, some physically impaired as their outer bodies decay with the passing of time, yet who are strong as steel on the inside; full of life and energy within. The love of Jesus burns deep within them and ignites the dying embers of our own life. Intimate communion with our living Lord is all about an inner inferno burning brightly for the things of God.

Strengthening the inner chambers of our life allows Christ to dwell in our hearts through faith. An interesting point can be made regarding the Greek word "dwell." There are two common words for "dwell" in the Bible. One is "katoikeo" and the other is "paroikeo." "Paroikeo" refers to a temporary dwelling place, and Paul uses this word in Ephesians 2:19 with reference to Christians as strangers and aliens, temporarily dwelling in this land. But in Ephesians 3:17, Paul informs us that Christ is to dwell (katoikeo) in our hearts by faith. This word refers to a permanent dwelling—a place that can be called home. The point is this: when we possess a robust inner strength through the mediating presence of the Holy Spirit, Jesus feels at home in our life.

Our continual inner communion with the Lord is the wellspring of life and a strong protection against the pressure toward irresponsible living. The reason so many believers do not finish the race is because they neglect inner communion with their Creator. Jesus doesn't fit into their life, and what they proclaim outwardly is not a reality inwardly. To finish well, especially with regard to relationships, maintain inner strength through intimate communion with God.

Discipline

Running all the way to the finish line also involves discipline of mind and body. To complete an endurance race, disciplined training is necessary. We don't just wake up the day of the race and decide to run the Boston Marathon. We wouldn't last unless we disciplined ourselves and trained for it. Many sprint out of the starting blocks of Christianity only to collapse within one hundred yards. Had the race been a sprint they may have done well, but Christianity isn't a fifty-yard dash; it is a marathon. Making it to the finish line involves keen discipline of mind and body.

In reality, "couch potato Christianity" is useless. We must take part in the preparation and running of the race. We don't rest on our laurels and say, "I'll just relax on the couch and let God do His thing." We are intimately involved in the process of growing and becoming more like Jesus, and this requires discipline and participation.

Things in life that are worthwhile always involve effort. Simply because I *want* to write a book or because I *feel* led to write a book, doesn't mean the book suddenly appears. I would love to write all kinds of books, but only those to which I devote time, discipline, and effort will ever find their way to printed pages. An enormous amount of creative energy is expended in writing. Preliminary research must be conducted, analyzed, sorted, and organized. Multiple rough drafts are produced, and extensive time is given to proofing the text. There are contracts to be negotiated, book covers to design, distribution avenues to consider, and so forth.

My point is this: choices must be made with one's time. Recently, a missionary to Africa shared how my first book was used in a group Bible study where twenty-four individuals came to follow Jesus. My choices with time, effort, and discipline paid off in spiritual returns that will forever bless me and others.

If you're like most people, you are probably disciplined in some areas of your life and not so disciplined in others. I am extremely disciplined in some parts of my life that have produced benefits to help me run the race. At the same time, I am keenly aware of the many areas where I am not as disciplined as I should be, or want to be. Yet, God's Spirit is working in me to harness these undisciplined quarters. Bringing discipline into our life is no easy task. Yet, if our goal is to run in such a way as to win, training is both essential and profitable. With the help of God's Spirit, discipline can turn our good intentions into tangible actions and living realities.

Running a marathon is an arduous task. Though it comes with significant joy and benefits, make no mistake about it, it is difficult work. Because we sometimes stumble and yearn to give up, it seems fitting to close with a poem entitled "The Race" by D. H. Groberg that inspires us to "keep on keepin on" until we reach the finish line and complete the race: [19]

THE RACE
D. H. Groberg

I.
"Quit! Give up! You're beaten!"
They shout at me and plead.
"There's just too much against you now.
This time you can't succeed!"

And as I start to hang my head
In front of failure's face,
My downward fall is broken by
The memory of a race.

And hope refills my weakened will
As I recall that scene;
For just the thought of that short race
Rejuvenates my being.

II.
A children's race—young boys, young men
How I remember well.
Excitement, sure! But also fear;
It wasn't hard to tell.

They all lined up so full of hope;
Each thought to win that race.
Or tie for first, or if not that,
At least take second place.

And fathers watched from off the side,
Each cheering for his son.
And each boy hoped to show his dad
That he would be the one.

The whistle blew and off they went!
Young hearts and hopes afire.
To win and be the hero there
Was each young boy's desire.

And one boy in particular
Whose dad was in the crowd,
Was running near the lead and thought,
"My dad will be so proud!"

But as they speeded down the field
Across a shallow dip,
The little boy who thought to win
Lost his step and slipped.

Trying hard to catch himself
His hands flew out to brace,
And mid the laughter of the crowd
He fell flat on his face.

So down he fell and with him hope
He couldn't win it now—
Embarrassed, sad, he only wished
To disappear somehow.

But as he fell his dad stood up
And showed his anxious face,
Which to the boy so clearly said:
"Get up and win the race."

He quickly rose, no damage done,
Behind a bit, that's all—
And ran with all his mind and might
To make up for his fall.

So anxious to restore himself
To catch up and to win—
His mind went faster than his legs;
He slipped and fell again!

He wished then he had quit before
With only one disgrace.
"I'm hopeless as a runner now;
I shouldn't try to race."

But in the laughing crowd he searched
And found his father's face.
That steady look which said again;
"Get up and win the race!"

So up he jumped to try again
Ten yards behind the last—
"If I'm to gain those yards," he thought,
"I've got to move real fast."

Exerting everything he had
He gained eight or ten
But trying so hard to catch the lead
He slipped and fell again!

Defeat! He lay there silently
A tear dropped from his eye—
"There's no sense running any more;
Three strikes: I'm out! Why try?"

The will to rise had disappeared
All hope had fled away;
So far behind, so error prone;
A loser all the way.

"I've lost, so what's the use," he thought
"I'll live with my disgrace."
But when he thought about his dad
Who soon he'd have to face.

"Get up," an echo sounded low.
"Get up and take your place;
You were not meant for failure here.
Get up and win the race.

"With borrowed will, get up," it said
"You haven't lost at all,
For winning is no more than this:
To rise each time you fall."

So up he rose to run once more,
And with a new commit
He resolved that win or lose
At least he wouldn't quit.

So far behind the others now,
The most he'd ever been—
Still he gave it all he had
And ran as though to win.

Three times he's fallen, stumbling;
Three times he rose again;
Too far behind to hope to win
He still ran to the end.

They cheered the winning runner
As he crossed the line first place,
Head high, and proud, and happy;
No falling, no disgrace.

But when the fallen youngster
Crossed the line last place,
The crowd gave him the greater cheer
For finishing the race.

And even though he came in last
With head bowed low, unproud,
You would have thought he'd won the
Race to listen to the crowd.

And to his dad he sadly said,
"I didn't do so well."
"To me, you won," his father said.
"You rose each time you fell."

III.
And now when things seem dark and hard
And difficult to face.
The memory of that little boy
Helps me in my own race.

For all of life is like that race.
With ups and downs and all.
And all you have to do to win,
Is rise each time you fall.

"Quit! Give up! You're beaten!"
They still shout in my face
But another voice within me says:
"GET UP AND WIN THE RACE."

My earnest prayer is that this book has benefitted you personally, professionally, and spiritually. You now understand the empowering effects of mentoring relationships. I implore you to invest your life in others as Jesus did with His disciples. Be a mentor to someone. Share with others what God has given to you, and by doing so, you will empower them to be the best they can be for the glory of God. Amen!

STUDY GUIDE QUESTIONS

1. Introduction
1. Provide an example of mentoring from your own life or an example you have observed in others.
2. Identify where the word "mentor" finds its origin.
3. Historically, where do we see mentoring woven throughout the biblical story? Provide examples and scriptural references.
4. As Mentor cared for Telemachus, describe how God acts as a mentor in the same four areas (protecting, guiding, nurturing, educating).

2. The Importance of Relationships
1. Discuss the relational transitions that have occurred in America and how they affect relationships.
2. Discuss the importance of relationships in the Bible. Be sure to include scriptural support.
3. Dr. Wise believes the learning process in our culture has shifted from being relationally based. Do you agree? Why or why not?
4. What three reasons are given for the renewed interest in mentoring? Can you think of other reasons?

3. What is Mentoring?
1. Define "mentoring" and discuss the three distinct components of the definition.
2. Is there a difference between discipleship and mentoring, or are they the same?
3. Can anyone mentor, or must one possess specific qualifications?

4. Mentoring in the Bible

1. Describe how Jesus mentored his disciples. Include the following areas: knowledge, values, leadership and direction, vulnerable situations, and trusting mentorees with skills and knowledge.
2. Describe the mentoring relationship between Moses and Joshua.
3. Why would Joshua not depart from the Tent of the Meeting?
4. Briefly state how Moses mentors Joshua even in the transition of power.
5. What are the striking parallels between Joshua's career and that of Moses?
6. Describe the mentoring relationship between Elijah and Elisha.
7. Describe the mentoring relationship between Paul and Timothy.

5. The Accountability Factor

1. Is America a good place for mentoring to occur? Why or why not?
2. Dr. Wise believes that accountability is all around us. Provide some common examples of this.
3. Why do individuals have more difficulty being accountable to others than to God?
4. The hardest aspect of accountability, as Dr. Wise suggests, is our *willingness* to be held accountable. Do you agree or disagree? Explain.
5. In your opinion, how does accountability benefit the mentoring relationship?
6. Do people usually do what we *inspect* or what we *expect*? Explain.
7. How does accountability in the wrong hands turn into an opportunity for criticism?
8. Provide a personal example of someone who tried to hold you accountable in the wrong way and without the right to do so. Provide a personal example where accountability was handled in the right manner and benefitted you.
9. List several verses that address the concept of accountability. For each passage cited, write a one-line sentence that sums up the teaching.

6. Influencing Others

1. Christians need a Barnabas, Timothy, and Epaphraditus in their life. What is meant by this, and how does it relate to mentoring?
2. Examine your own life; do you have a Barnabas, Timothy, and Epaphraditus?
3. Everyone has been influenced by someone. Discuss the value of a positive example.
4. Why is it important to see potential in others, and how does this relate to mentoring?

5. Explain the significance of patience and tolerance in the mentoring relationship.
6. Why is encouragement essential to the mentoring relationship?
7. Explain the relevance of mentors seeing the big picture.
8. How can being a "resource guide" benefit the mentoring relationship?
9. Explain why mentors who are too busy hinder the relationship, and distinguish between being busy and being *too* busy.
10. Explain why finding mentors who want to help you, not use you, is essential.
11. Why is it imperative to avoid mentors who criticize?
12. Why is it crucial to avoid mentors who are "not with the times?"

7. Mentors and Mentorees
1. List and describe several characteristics to look for when selecting a mentor.
2. List and describe several characteristics to look for when selecting a mentoree.
3. What are the three vital dynamics of mentoring, and how do they relate to the success of the relationship?

8. Levels of Mentoring
1. List and describe the three different levels of mentoring.
2. Why are the three vital dynamics more weighty in the intensive level than other levels?
3. Describe the role of discipler as found in the intensive level.
4. List and discuss four reasons why so many in our churches yearn for mentoring relationships.
5. Describe the role of spiritual guide as found in the intensive level.
6. How does the discipler differ from the spiritual guide?
7. When might you seek out an individual to be a spiritual guide?
8. Describe the role of coach as found in the intensive level.
9. Discuss how observation, feedback, and evaluation is helpful in the coaching role. Provide a personal example of how someone acting as coach used these three steps to help you.
10. Describe the role of counselor as found in the occasional level.
11. List several passages that relate to the concept of gathering wise counsel.
12. What problems might arise when receiving counsel from someone *too* close to the situation?
13. Describe the role of teacher as found in the occasional level.
14. Describe the role of sponsor as found in the occasional level.

15. Does sponsoring leave God's sovereignty out of the equation in helping others? Explain.
16. Dr. Wise believes that potential leaders either fall between the cracks or are lost to other organizations when sponsoring does not occur. Do you agree or disagree? Explain.
17. Why is modeling a biblical concept?
18. Describe the contemporary and historical models of mentoring. Provide a personal example of each from your own life.

9. Practical Helps
1. Why is balance in one's life so critical with regard to mentoring?
2. List and discuss the three dimensions of a balanced relational network of accountability.
3. Do you find this balance in your own life? Explain.
4. Describe the close friendship between David and Jonathan as seen in I Samuel.
5. What can we learn from those who have walked the path of mentoring before us?
6. How can mentoring occur in the home?
7. How is the church a fertile environment for routine mentoring?
8. Do books have the ability to mentor? Explain.

10. Expanding the Blessing
1. List and discuss the three key attitudes learned from the study of healthy CEOs and why they are significant.
2. What other items did the study of healthy CEOs discover?
3. How can the study of CEOs be applied to the spiritual realm?
4. Discuss the concept of communion with God as it relates to one's perseverance to the end.
5. Why is discipline essential to finishing the race set before us?
6. Examine your own life. What areas need improvement if you are to finish the race and persevere to the end?

ENDNOTES

1. Bob Biehl, *Mentoring* (Nashville, TN: Broadman & Holman, 1996), 11.
2. US Department of Energy, *Mentoring Program Guide*, May 1996, 3.
3. Webster's Encyclopedic Unabridged Dictionary (Avenel, NJ: Random House, 1996), 1201.
4. Health Care Financing Administration, *Mentoring Momentum Newsletter*, Spring 1998, 1.
5. Ted Engstrom, *The Fine Art of Mentoring* (Brentwood, TN: Wolgemuth & Hyatt, 1989), 4.
6. Biehl, *Mentoring*, 19.
7. Paul Stanley & Robert Clinton, *Connecting* (Colorado Springs, CO: Navpress, 1992), 33.
8. Engstrom, *The Fine Art of Mentoring*, 43. The quote is by John Crosby as found in Engstrom's book.
9. Ibid., 21.
10. Hellen Kellor, *The Story of My Life* (New York, NY: Doubleday, Page & Co., 1905), 311.
11. Engstrom, *The Fine Art of Mentoring*, 27.
12. Ibid., 43.
13. Robert Coleman, *The Master Plan of Evangelism* (Grand Rapids, MI: Spire, 1994), 29.
14. Stanley & Clinton, *Connecting*, 43–44.

15. The three levels of mentoring and the various categories of involvement in each level forms the basis of Paul Stanley and Robert Clinton's book *Connecting*.
16. *Leadership Journal*, Vol. 14, No. 2, Spring 1993, 89.
17. Stanley & Clinton, *Connecting*, 159–167.
18. Biehl, *Mentoring*, 163–167.
19. Source uncertain. Printed in Stanley & Clinton's book *Connecting*.

SELECTED BIBLIOGRAPHY

Alleman, E. *Measuring Mentoring-Frequency, Quality, Impact*. In Proceedings of the First International Conference in Mentoring, Vol. 2. W. A. Gray and M.M. Gray (eds.). Vancouver, British Columbia, Canada: International Association of Mentoring, 1986, 51.

_____. "Mentoring Relationships in Organizations: Behaviors, Personality Characteristics, and Interpersonal Perceptions," *Dissertation Abstracts International* (1982): 43:75A.

_____. Two Planned Mentoring Programs that Worked. *Mentoring International* 3 (1) 1989, 6–12.

Alleman, E., Cochran, J., Doverspike, J., and Newman, 1. "Enriching Mentoring Relationships," *The Personnel and Guidance Journal* 62(6) (1984): 329–32.

Anderson, E.M., and Shannon, A.L. "Toward a Conceptualization of Mentoring," *Journal of Teacher Education* 39(1) (1988): 38–42.

Anderson, R., and Ramey, P. *Women in Higher Education: Development through Administrative Mentoring*. In L. Welch (ed.) Women in Higher Education-Changes and Challenges. New York: Praeger, 1990, 183–190.

Appel, M., and Trail, T. *Building Effective Professional Adult Education Mentoring*. In Proceedings of the First International Conference on Mentoring, Vol. 1. W.A. Gray And M.M. Gray (eds). Vancouver, British Columbia, Canada: International Association for Mentoring, 1986, 63–70.

Bahniuk, M., Dobos, J., and Hill, S. "The Impact of Mentoring, Collegial Support, and Information Adequacy on Career Success: A Replication," *Journal of Social Behavior and Personality* 5(4) (1990): 431–51.

Barnett, B. "The Mentor-Intern Relationship: Making the Most of Learning from Experience," *NASSP Bulletin* 74 (1990): 17–24.

Bell, Chip R. Managers As Mentors: *Building Partnership for Learning*. Berrett-Koehler Publishing, 1998.

Biehl, B., and Urquhart, G. *Mentoring: How to Find a Mentor, How to Be One*. Laguna Niguel, CA: Masterplanning Group, 1990.

_____. *Mentoring*. Boradman & Holman, Nashville, TN, 1996.

Bolton, E. "A Conceptual Analysis of the Mentor Relationship in Career Development of Women," *Adult Education* 30(4) (1980): 195–207.

Borman, C., and Colson, S. "Mentoring: An Effective Career Guidance Technique," *Vocational Guidance Quarterly* 32(3) (1984): 192–197.

Bova, B.M., and Phillips, R.R. "The Mentor Relationship: A Study of Mentors and Protégé in Business and Academia," *ERIC Document Reproduction Service* (1981): No. 208 233.

_____. "Mentoring as a Learning Experience for Adults," *Journal of Teacher Education* 35(3) (1984): 16–20.

Bowen, D. "Were Men Meant to Mentor Women?" *Training and Development Journal* 39(2) (1985): 31–36.

Burke, R., and McKeen, C. "Mentoring in Organizations: Implications for Women," *Journal of Business Ethics* 9 (1990): 317–332.

Cahill, M.F., and Kelly, J.J. "A Mentor Program for Nursing Majors," *Journal of Nursing Education* (1989): 28:40–42.

Cain, R. "Critical Incidents and Critical Requirements in Mentoring," *Journal of Non-Traditional Studies* 16(2) (1989): 111–127.

Carmin, C.N. "Issues in Research on Mentoring: Definitional and Methodological," *International Journal of Mentoring* 2(2) (1988): 9–13.

Caruso, R. *Mentoring and the Business Environment—Asset or Liability?* Brookfield, VT: Dartmouth Publishing Company, 1992.

Clawson, J. "Is Mentoring Necessary?" *Training and Development Journal* 39(4) (1985): 36–39.

Clawson, J.G., and Kram, K.E. "Managing Cross-Gender Mentoring." *Business Horizons*, 1984, 27:22–32.

Clinton, J., and Clinton, R. *The Mentor Handbook: Detailed Guidelines and Helps for Christian Mentors and Mentorees*. Altadena, CA: Barnabas Publishers, 1991.

Collin, A. *The Role of the Mentor in the Experience of Change*. In Proceedings of the First International Conference on Mentoring, Vol. 2. W.A. Gray and M.M. Gray (eds.). Vancouver, British Columbia, Canada: International Association for Mentoring, 1986, 94–101.

Collins, E.G.D., and Scott, P. "Everyone Who Makes it Has a Mentor," *Harvard Business Review* (July-Aug 1978): 89–101.

Crosby, L. *How to Bring Mentor and Protégé Together–Formally*. In Report 1564, Sec. 1: Bureau of Business Practice. Waterford, CT: National Foremen's Institute 1984.

Daloz, L.A. *Effective Teaching and Mentoring*. San Francisco: Jossey-Bass Publishers, 1986.

Darling, L.A.W. Endings in Mentor Relationships. *The Journal of Nursing Administration* 15(11), (1985): 40–41.

_____. "What Do Nurses Want in a Mentor?" *The Journal of Nursing Administration*. (October 1984): 42–44.

_____. "Mentor Matching," *The Journal of Nursing Administration*. (January 1985a): 45–46.

_____. "Mentors and Mentoring." *The Journal of Nursing Administration* (March 1985b): 42–43.

Dreher, G., and Ash, R. "A Comparative Study of Mentoring Among Men and Women in Managerial, Professional, and Technical Positions," *Journal of Applied Psychology* 75(5) (1990): 539–546.

Egan, J.B. *Characteristics of Mentor Teachers' Mentor-Protégé Relationships*. In Proceedings of the First International Conference on Mentoring, Vol. 1. W.A. Gray and M.M. Gray (eds.). Vancouver, British Columbia, Canada: International Association for Mentoring, 1986, 55–62.

Engstrom, Ted. *The Fine Art of Mentoring*. Brentwood, Wolgemuth & Hyatt, 1989.

Erkut, E., and Mokros, J. "Professors as Models and Mentors for College Students," *American Educational Research Journal* 21(2) (1984): 399–417.

Fagan, M.M. *Do Formal Mentoring Programs Really Mentor?* In Proceedings of the First International Conference on Mentoring, Vol. 2. W.A. Gray and M.M. Gray (eds). Vancouver, British Columbia, Canada: International Association for Mentoring, 1986 23–43.

Fagan, M.M., and Walters, G. "Mentoring Among Teachers," *Journal of Educational Research* 7(2) (1982): 113–117.

Fagenson, E. "Mentoring-Who Needs it? A Comparison of Protégé and Non-Protégé Needs for Power, Achievement, Affiliation and Autonomy," *Journal of Vocational Behavior* 41 (1992): 48–60.

Fagenson, F. "The Mentor Advantage: Perceived Career/Job Experiences of Protégés Versus Non-Protégés," *Journal of Organizational Behavior* 10 (1989): 309–320.

Farren, C., Gray, J., and Kaye, B. "Mentoring: A Boon to Career Development." Personnel Journal 61(6) (1984): 20–24.

Fitt, L., and Newton, D. "When the Mentor Is a Man and the Protégé is a Woman," *Harvard Business Review* 59(2) (1981): 56–60.

Flaxman, E. *Good Mentoring.* In The Power of Mentoring. New York: One PLUS One, 1990.

Frey, B., and Nollar, R. "Mentoring: A Promise for the Future," *Journal of Creative Behavior* 20(1) (1986): 49–51.

Galbraith, Michael W., and Cohen, Norman H. (eds.) *Mentoring: New Strategies and Challenges.* (No. 66) Jossey-Bass Publishers. San Francisco, 1995.

_____. "Mentoring Among Teachers: A Review of the Literature," *Journal of Teacher Education.* 37(1) (1986): 6–11.

Gaskill, L. " Same-sex and Cross-sex Mentoring of Female Protégés: A Comparative Analysis," *The Career Development Quarterly* 40 (1991): 48–63.

Gehrke, N., and Kay, R. "The Socialization of Beginning Teachers through Mentor-protégé Relationships," *Journal of Teacher Education* 35(3) (1984): 21–24.

Gray, W.A., and Gray, M.M. (eds.). *Mentoring: A Comprehensive Annotated Bibliography of Important References*. Vancouver, British Columbia, Canada: International Association for Mentoring, 1986.

Groder, M.G. Everything You Want to Know About Mentors (Condensed). *Boardroom Reports*, 1980, 10, 5.

Hamlin, K., and Hering, K. "Help for the First-Year Teacher: Mentor, Buddy, or Both?" *NASSP Bulletin* 72(509) (1988): 125–127.

Haring-Hidore, M. "Mentoring as a Career Enhancement Strategy for Women," *Journal of counseling and Development* 66 (1987): 147–148.

Head, F., and Gray, M.M. The Legacy of Mentor: Insights into Western History, Literature and the Media. *International Journal of Mentoring*, 2(2) 1988, 26–33.

Hendricks, Howard G., and William D. *As Iron Sharpens Iron*. Chicago: Moody Press, 1995.

Horgan, B. How to Be a Mentor. *Kiwanis Magazine*, 69 1984, 25–28, 47.

Horgan, D., and Simeon, R. "Gender, Mentoring, and Tacit Knowledge," *Journal of Social Behavior and Personality* 5(4) (1990): 453–471.

Huang, Chungliang Al. *Mentoring: the Tao of Giving and Receiving Wisdom*. Harper Publishing. San Francisco, 1995.

Hughes, B. The Corporate Mentor. *Republic Scene*, Oct. 1980. 50–57.

Hunt, D.A. *Formal vs. Informal Mentoring: Toward a Framework*. In Proceedings of the First International Conference on Mentoring, Vol. 2. W.A. Gray and M.M. Gray (eds.). Vancouver, British Columbia, Canada: International Association for Mentoring, 1986, 8–14.

Kram, K. *Mentoring in the Workplace*. In D. Hall and Associates (eds.) Career Development in Organizations. San Francisco: Jossey-Bass, 1986, 160–201.

_____. *Mentoring at Work: Developmental Relationships in Organizational Life*. Lanham, MD: University Press of America, 1988.

_____. "Phases of Mentor Relationship," *Academy of Management Journal* 26(4) (1983): 608–625.

_____. "Improving the Mentoring Process," *Training and Development Journal* 39(4) (1985): 40–43.

Lageman, A. "Myths, Metaphors, and Mentors," *Journal of Religion and Health* 25(1) (1986): 58–63.

Mentoring Momentum. Health Care Financing Administration, Spring 1998.

Mentoring Program Guide. U. S. Department of Energy, May 1996.

Merriam, W. Mentors and Protégés: A Critical Review of the Literature. *Adult Education Quarterly* 1983, 33(3): 161–73.

Milan, C. *The Learning Autobiography: A Foundation for Mentoring*. In New Directions for Adult and Continuing Education. San Francisco: Jossey-Bass, 1990, 59–63.

Moore, K.M. "The Role of Mentors in Developing Leaders for Academe," *Educational Record* 6(1) (1982): 23–28.

Murray, M. *Beyond the Myths and Magic of Mentoring: How to Facilitate an Effective Mentoring Program*. San Francisco: Jossey-Bass, 1991.

Myers, D.W.., and Humphreys, N.J. The Caveats in Mentorship. *Business Horizons*, 28 1985, 9–14.

Noeller, R. "Mentoring: A Renaissance of Apprenticeship," *Journal of Creative Behavior* 16(1) (1982): 1–4.

Osterhaus, James. *Bonds of Iron: Forging Lasting Male Relationships*. Chicago: Moody Press, 1994.

Phillips-Jones, L. "Establishing a Formalized Mentoring Program," *Training and Development Journal* 37(2) (1983): 38–42.

_____. *Mentors and Protégés*. New York: Arbor House, 1982.

Ragins, B., and Cotton, J. "Easier Said than Done: Gender Differences in Perceived Barriers to Gaining a Mentor," *Academy of Management Journal* 34(4) (1991): 939–951.

Rawlins, M., and Rawlins, L. "Mentoring and Networking for Helping Professionals," *Personnel and Guidance Journal* 61(2) (1983): 116–118.

Roche, G. "Much Ado About Mentors," *Harvard Business Review* 57(1) (1979): 14–28.

Sands, R., Parson, L., and Duane, J. "Faculty Mentoring Faculty in a Public University." *Journal of Higher Education* 62(2) (1991): 174–193.

Scandura, T. "Mentorship and Career Mobility: An Empirical Investigation," *Journal of Organizational Behavior* 13 (1992): 169–174.

Serlen, B. "How Mentoring Programs Work," *Journal of Career Planning and Employment* 49 (1989): 54–56.

Shandley, T.C. "The Use of Mentors for Leadership Development," *NASPA Journal* 27(1) (1989): 59–66.

Shapiro, F., Hasentine, F., and Rowe, M. "Moving Up: Role Models, Mentors, and the Patron System," Sloan *Management Review* 19 (1978): 51–58.

Spruance, F. *Mentoring Manual*. Dresher, PA: Conservative Baptist Seminary of the East, 1992.

Stanley, P., and Clinton, J. *Connecting: The Mentoring Relationships You Need to Succeed in Life*. Colorado Springs: NavPress, 1992.

Sullivan, R., and Miklas, D. "On-the job Training that Works," *Training and Development Journal* 39(5) (1985): 118–120.

Torrance, P. *Mentor Relationships: How they Aid Creative Achievement, Endure, Change, and Die*. Buffalo, NY: Bearly Limited, 1984.

Whitely, W., Dougherty, T., and Dreher, G. "Correlates of Career Oriented Mentoring for Early Career Managers and Professionals," *Journal of Organizational Behavior* 13 (1992): 141–154.

_____. "Relationship of Career Mentoring and Social Economic Origin to Managers and Professionals Early Career Progress," *Academy of Management Journal* 34(2) (1991): 331–351.

Wilbur, J. "Does Mentoring Breed Success?," *Training and Development Journal* 41(11) (1987): 38–41.

Woodlands Group. "Management Development Roles: Coach, Sponsor, and Mentor," *Personnel Journal* 59(11) (1980): 918–921.

Wunsch, Marie, ed. *Mentoring Revisited: Making an Impact on Individuals and Institutions*. San Francisco, Jossey-Bass, No. 57, Spring 1994.

Zey, M. "Mentor Programs: Making the Right Moves," *Personnel Journal* 64(2) (1985): 53–57.

_____. *The Mentor Connection: Strategic Alliances in Corporate Life*. New Brunswick: Transaction Publishers, 1991.

www.ingramcontent.com/pod-product-compliance
Lightning Source LLC
Chambersburg PA
CBHW050636300426
44112CB00012B/1826